# Silhouette Handbook
## of
# UNITED STATES
# ARMY AIR FORCES
# Airplanes

Compiled by:
The Office of the Chief of Ordnance
Washington D.C.

ISBN 1 85520 5505

BROOKLANDS BOOKS LTD.
P.O. BOX 146, COBHAM,
SURREY, KT11 1LG.  UK
sales@brooklands-books.com  &  TIME ROVER PRESS
40124 LONE OAK ROAD
ZION, ILLINOIS 60099-958
DaleDRR@aol.com

A-MVSAA

Printed in Hong Kong

# SILHOUETTE
## Handbook
## of
# UNITED STATES
# ARMY AIR FORCES
## Airplanes

NOTICE: This document contains information affecting the National Defense of the United States within the meaning of the Espionage Act (U.S.C. 50:31:32). The transmission of this document or the revelation of its contents in any manner to an unauthorized person is prohibited.

*PUBLISHED BY AUTHORITY OF THE COMMANDING GENERAL, ARMY AIR FORCES, BY THE CHIEF, FIELD SERVICES, AIR SERVICE COMMAND, WRIGHT FIELD, DAYTON, OHIO.*

SEPTEMBER 1942

# CONTENTS

103'-10"
73'-10"
Boeing B-17E

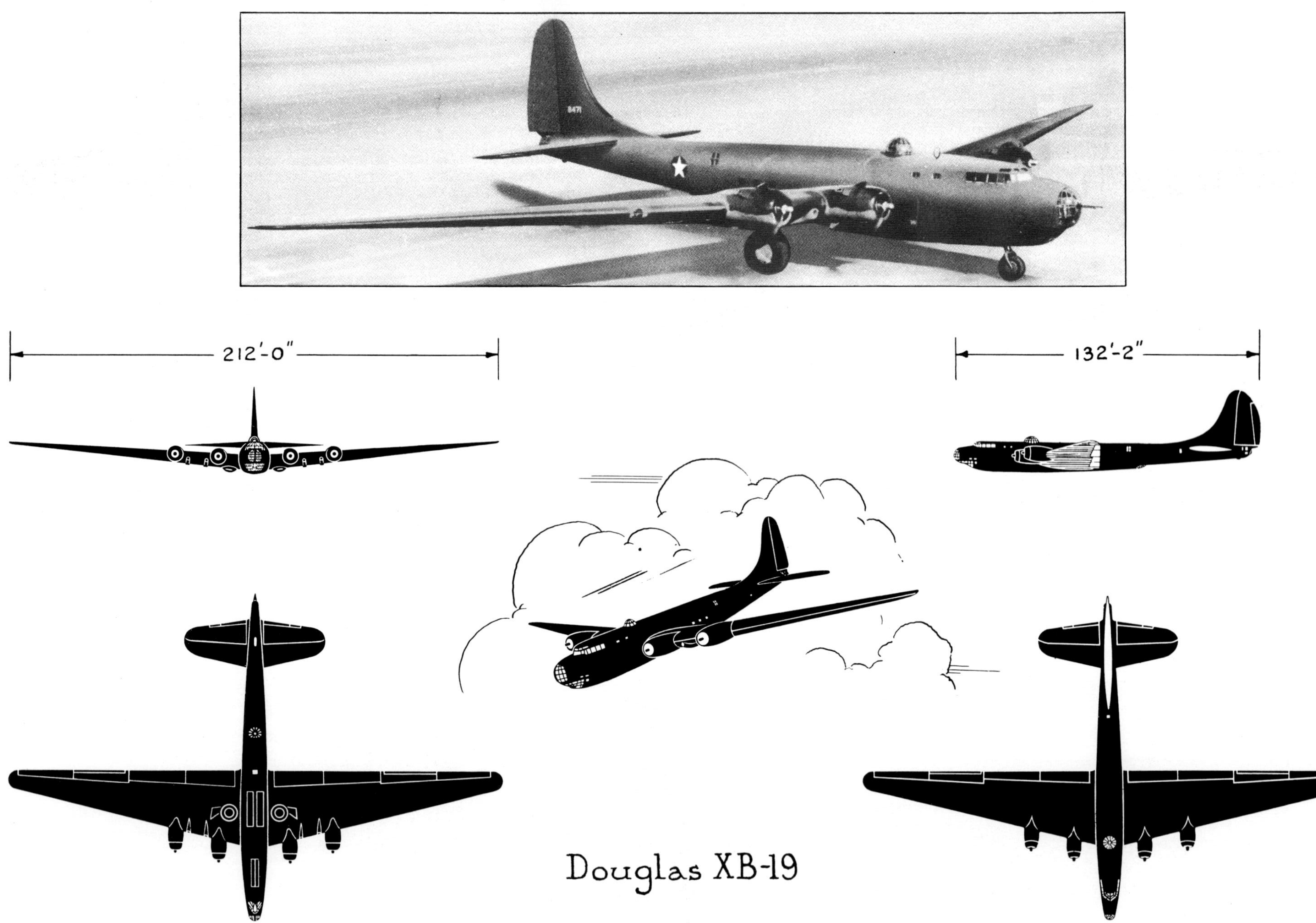
212'-0"
132'-2"
Douglas XB-19

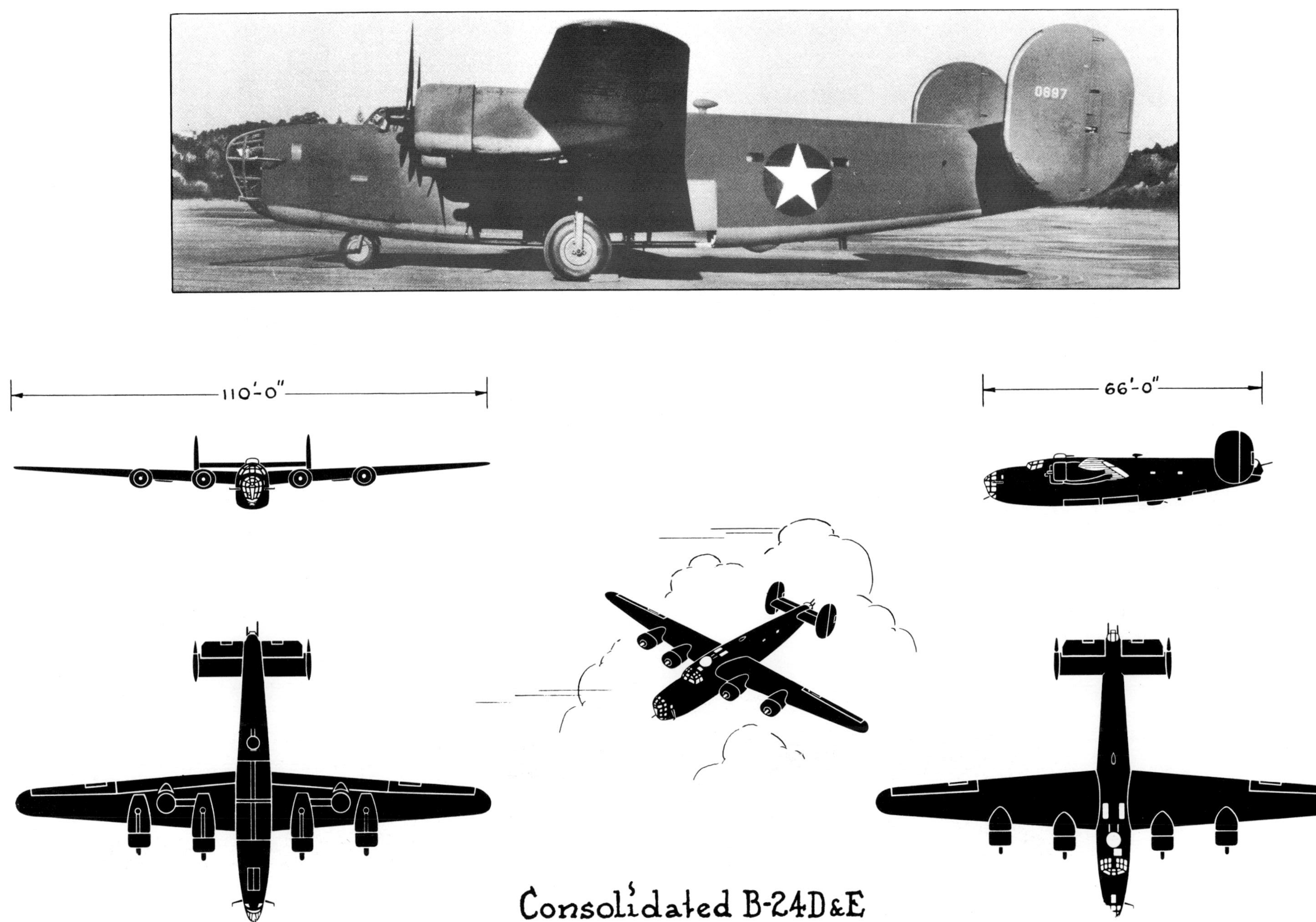

110'-0"
66'-0"
Consolidated B-24D&E

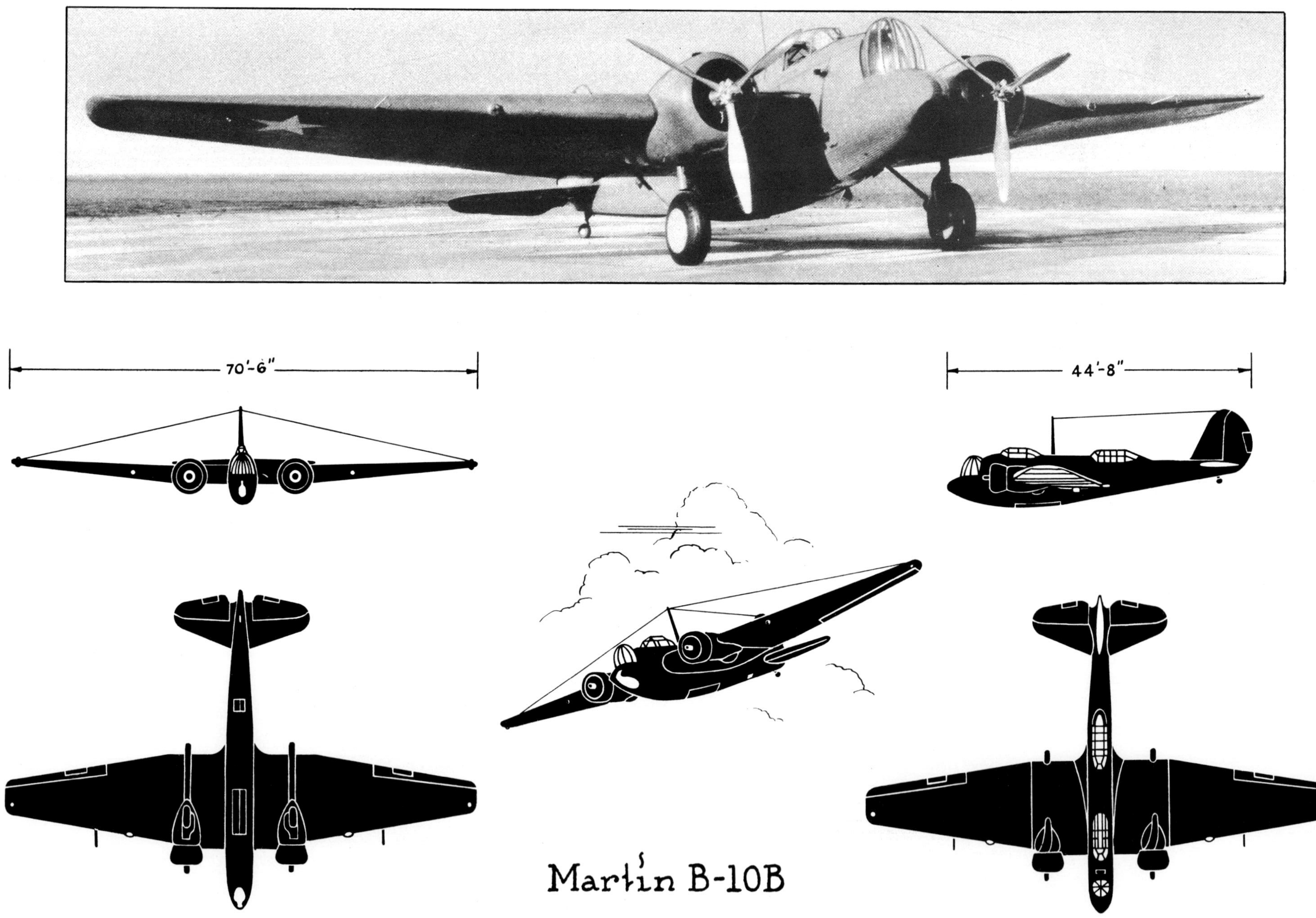

70'-6"
44'-8"
Martin B-10B

89'-6"
56'-8"
Douglas B-18

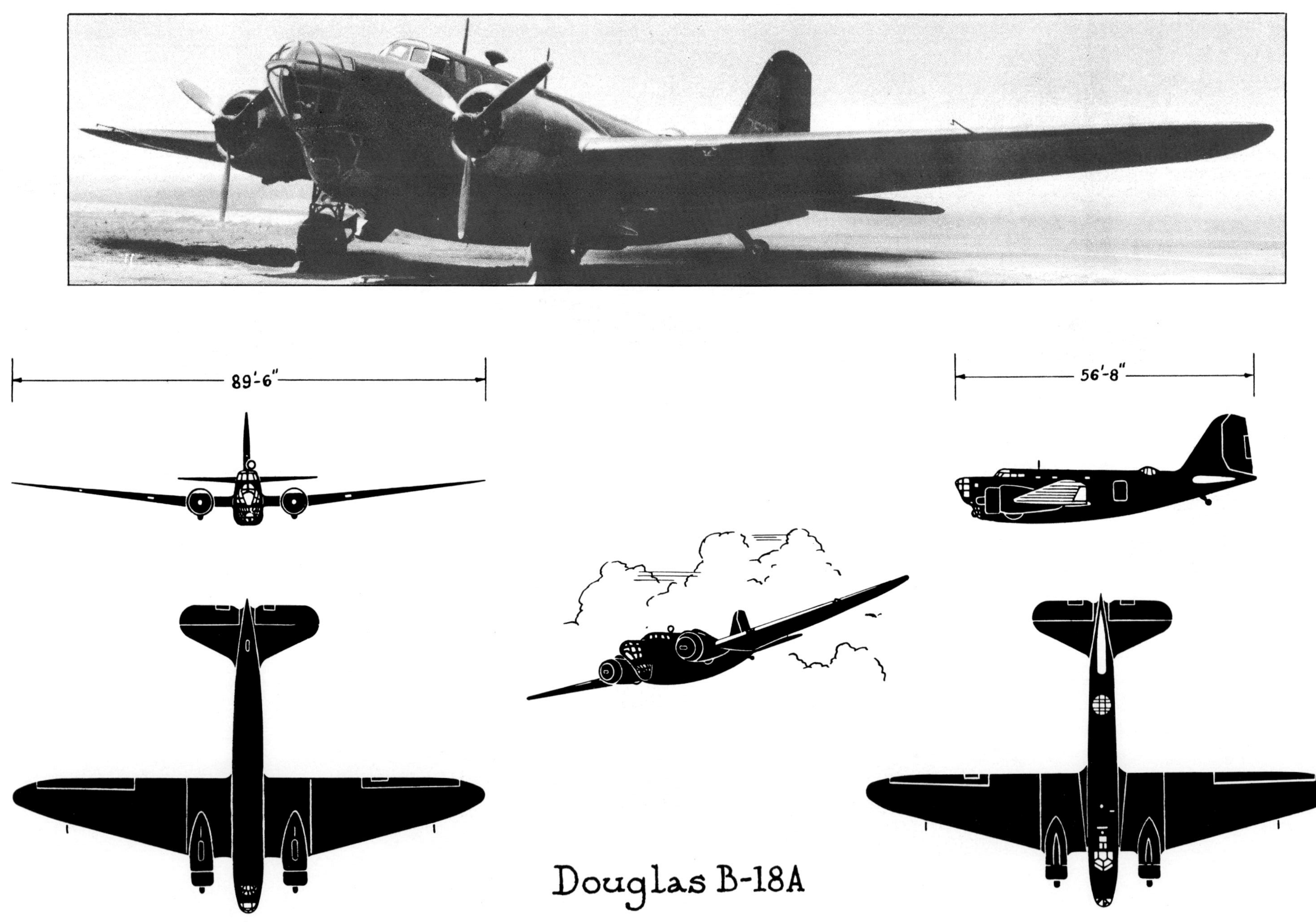


89'-6"
56'-8"
Douglas B-18A

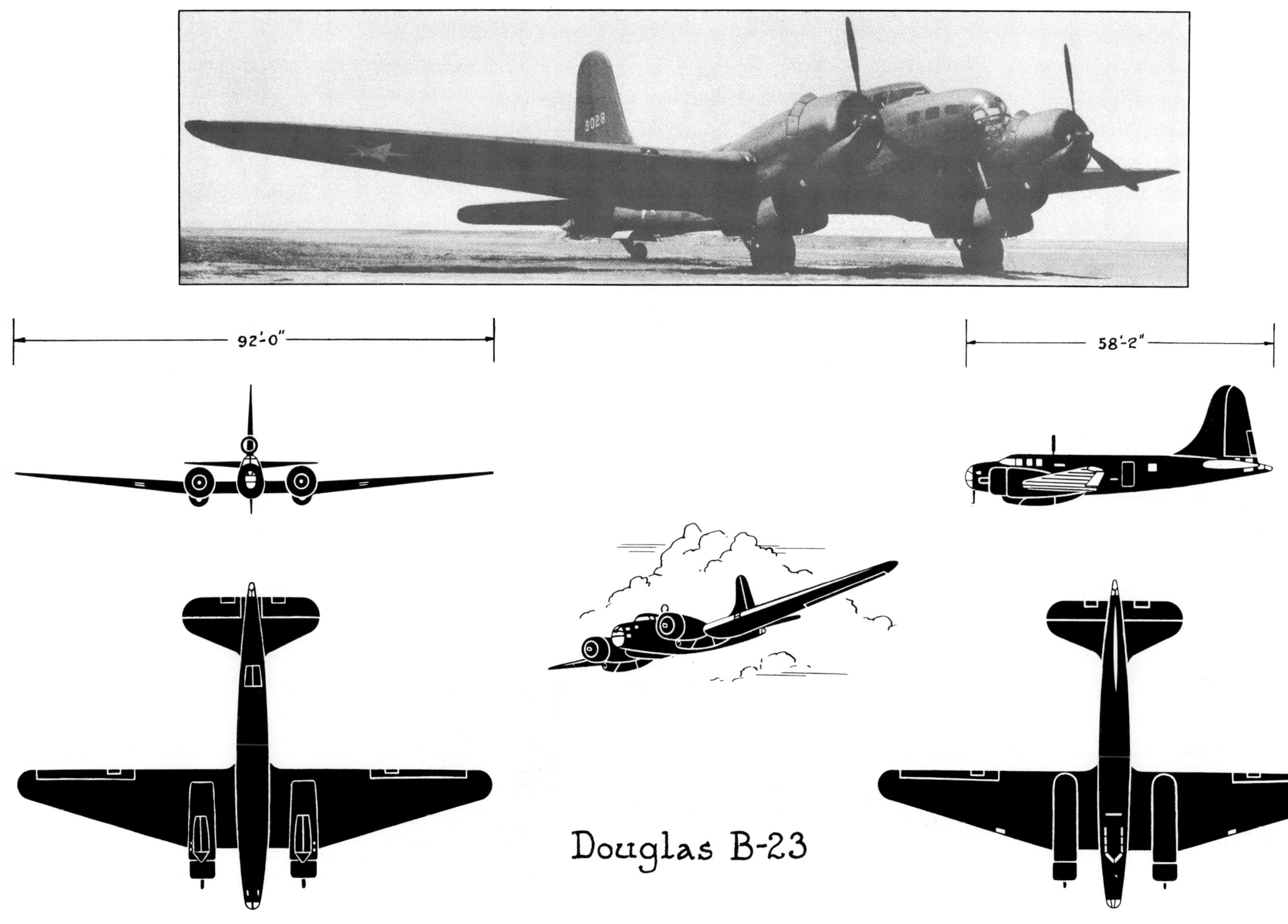
92'-0"
58'-2"
Douglas B-23

67'-6"
54'-0"
North American B-25C&D

65'-0"
58'-3"
Martin B-26B&C

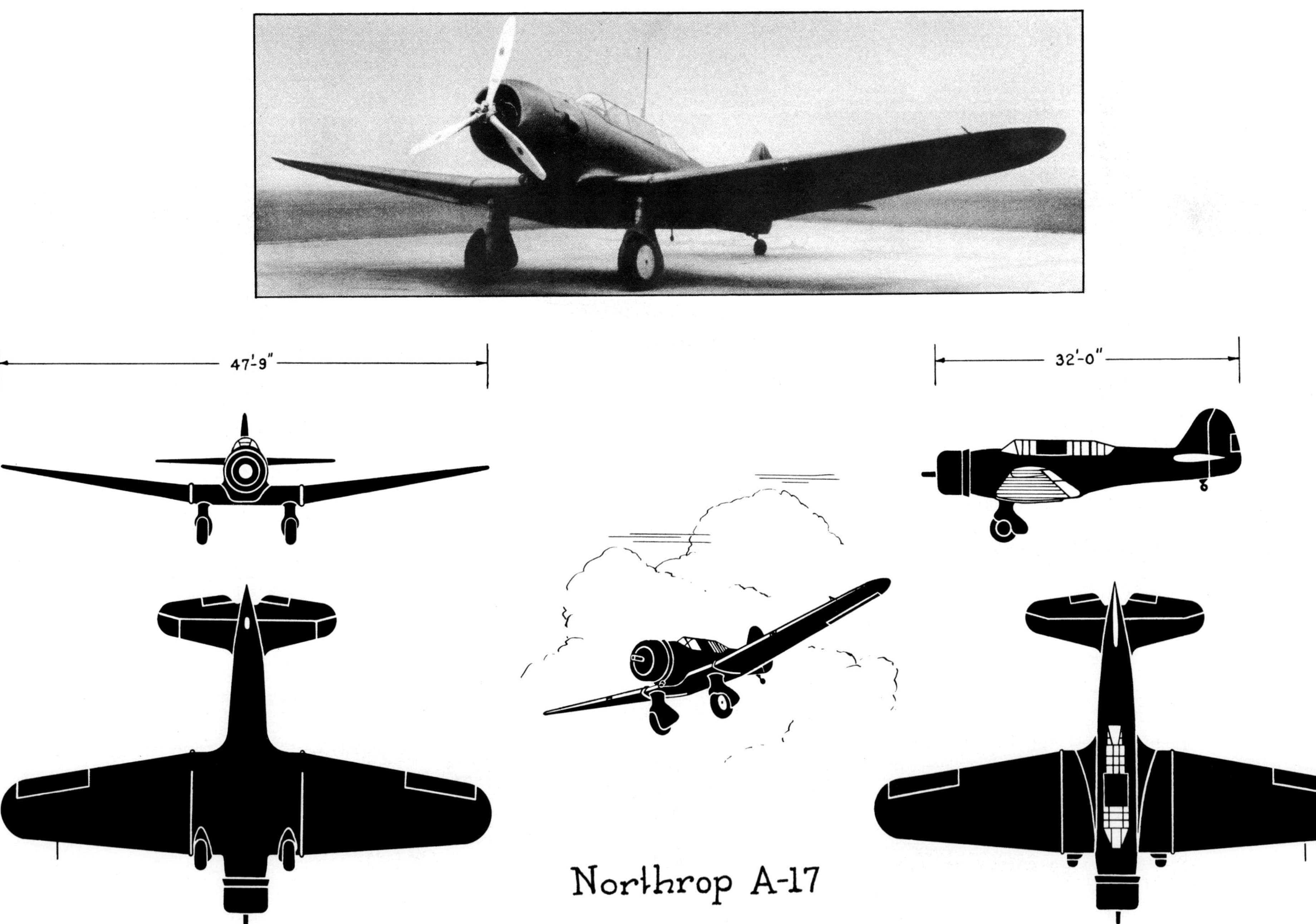

47'-9"
32'-0"
Northrop A-17

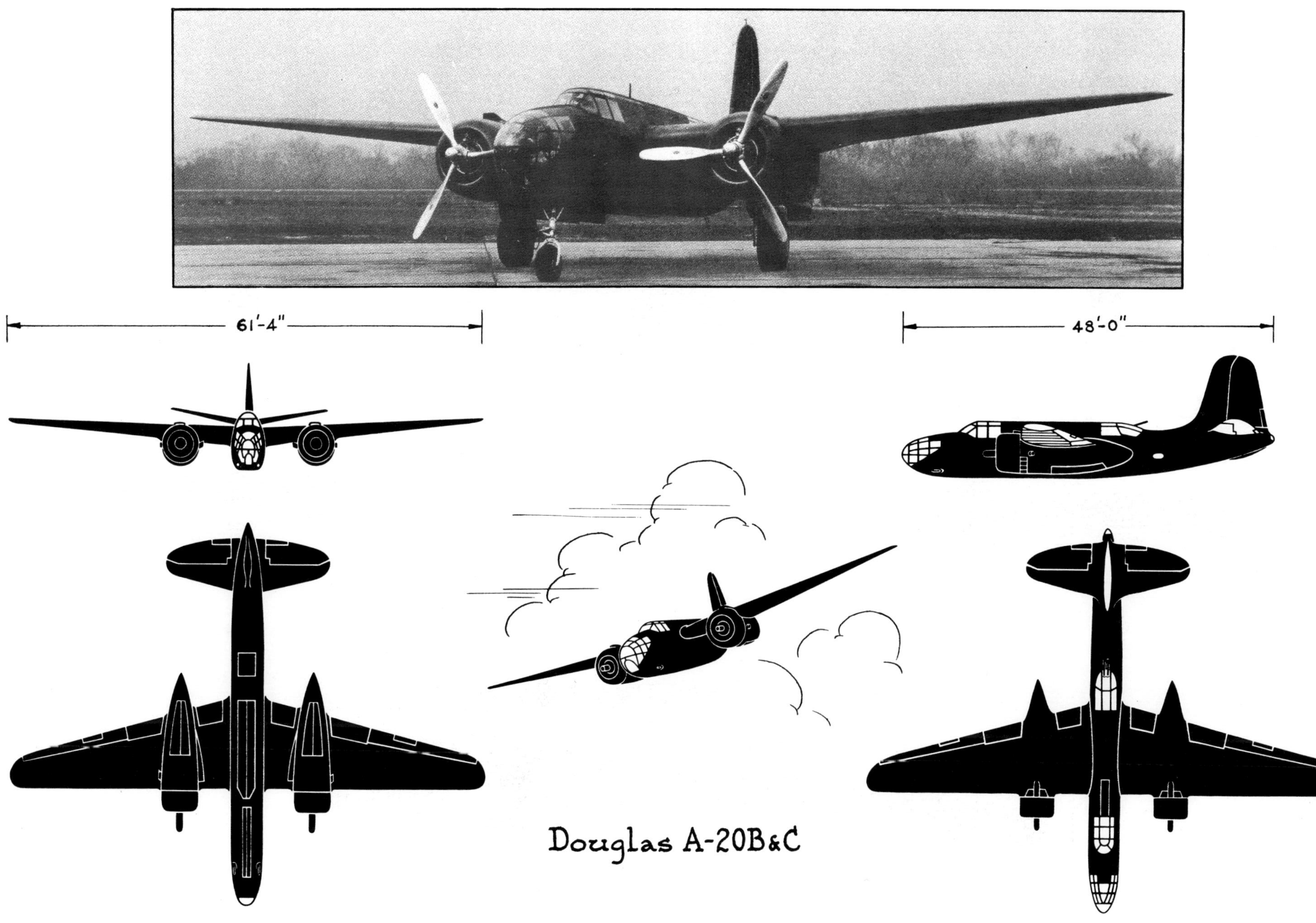

61'-4"
48'-0"
Douglas A-20B&C

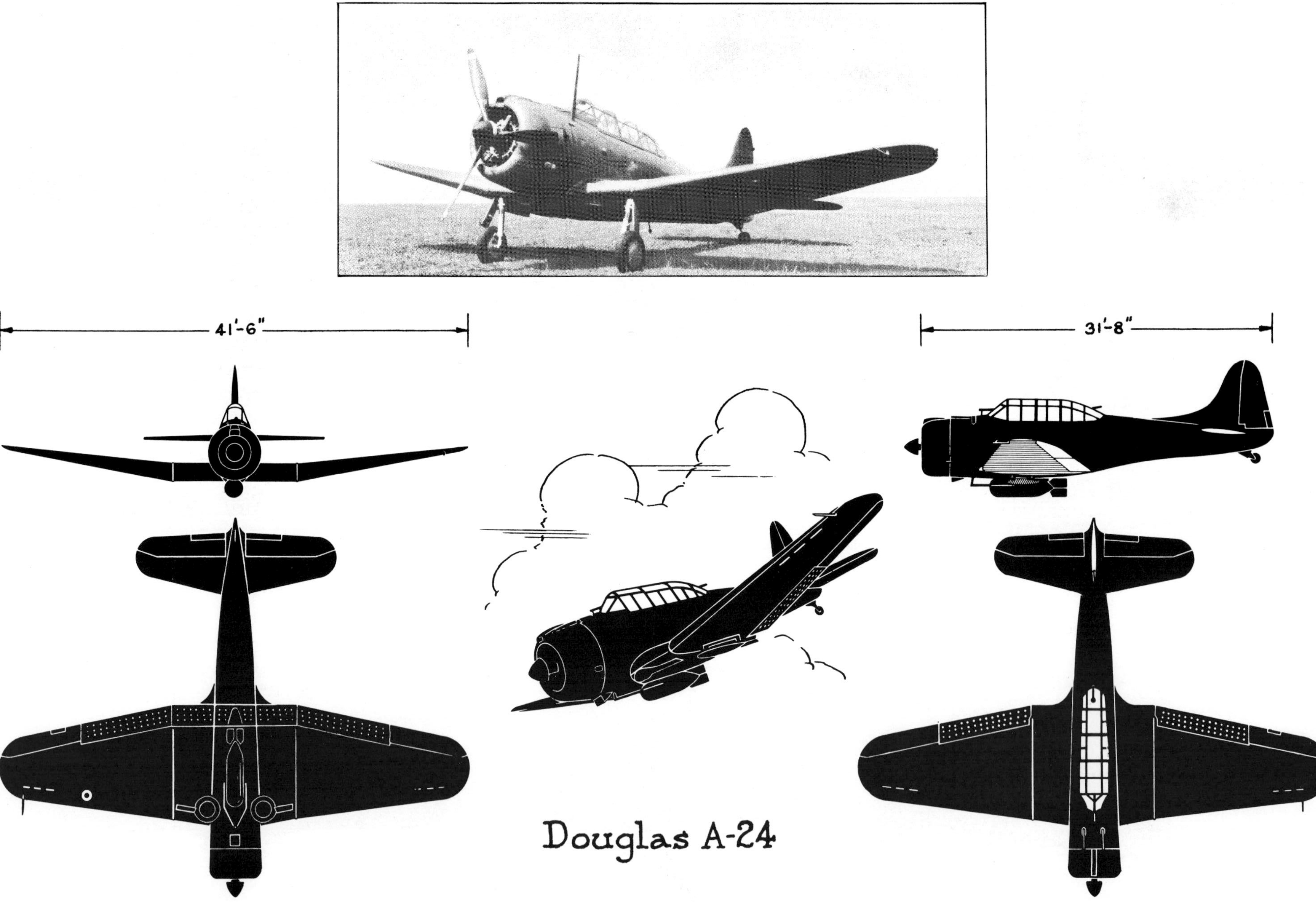

41'-6"
31'-8"
Douglas A-24

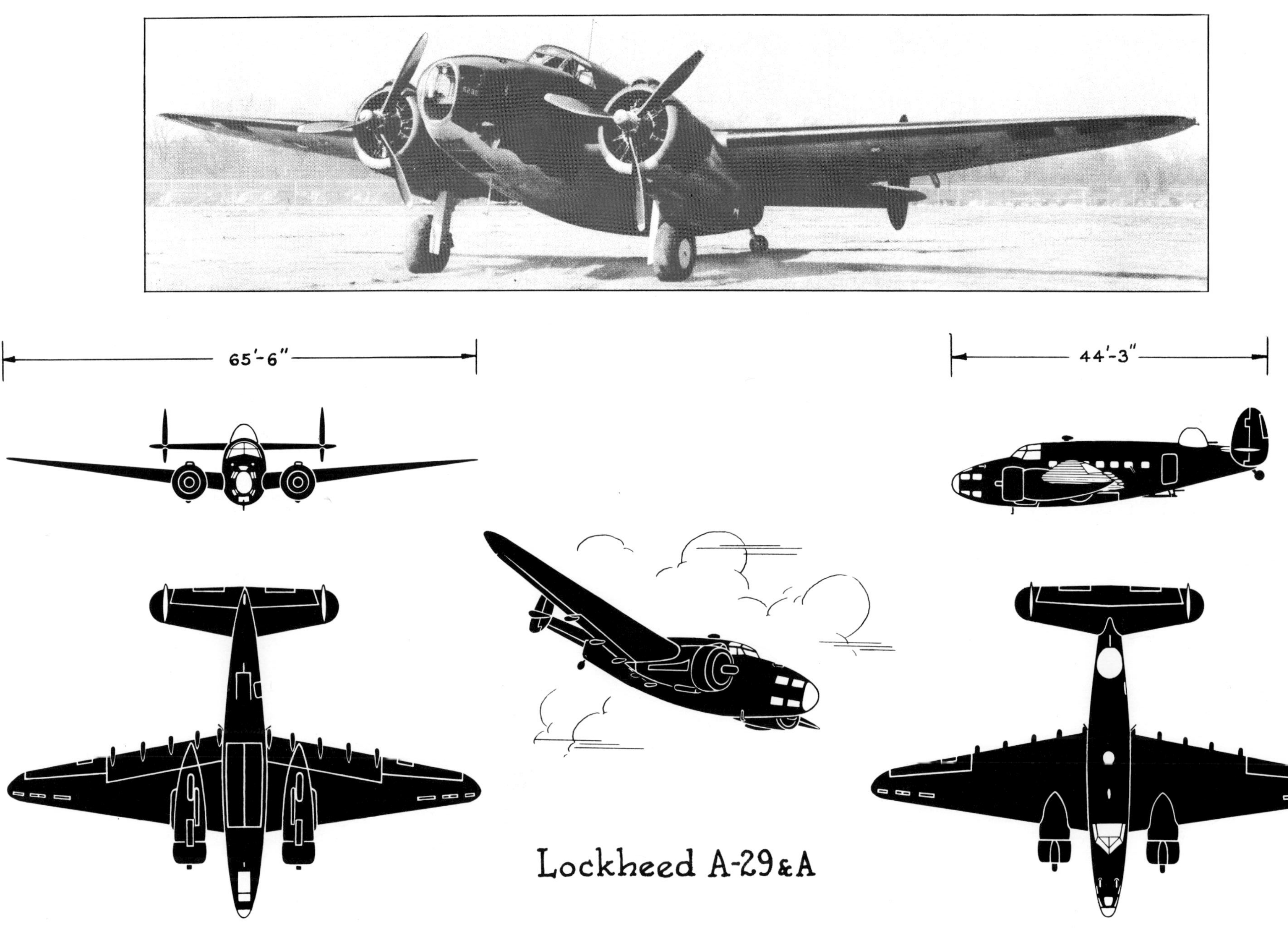


65'-6"
44'-3"
Lockheed A-29&A

61'-4"
48'-6"
Martin A-30

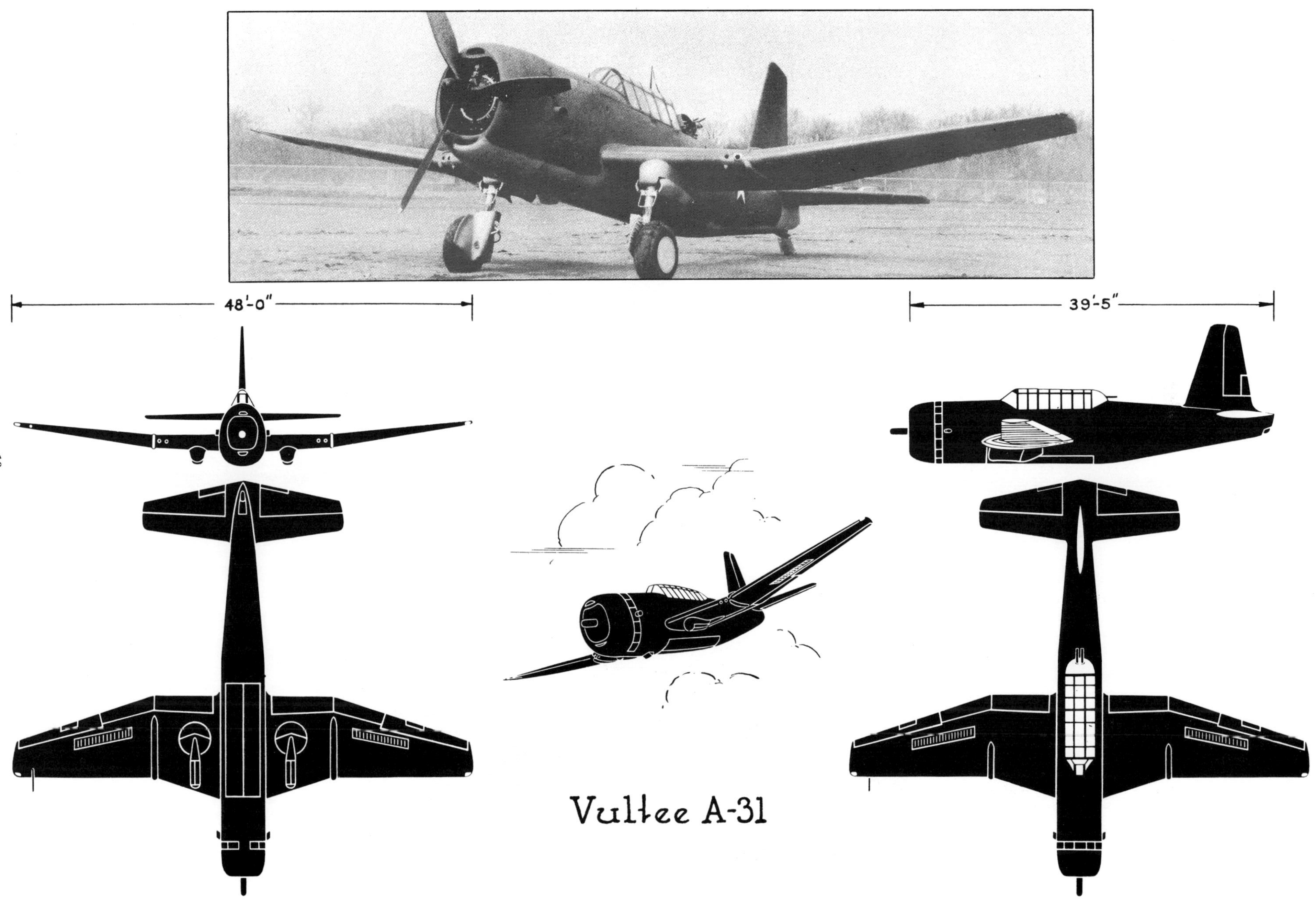


48'-0"
39'-5"
Vultee A-31

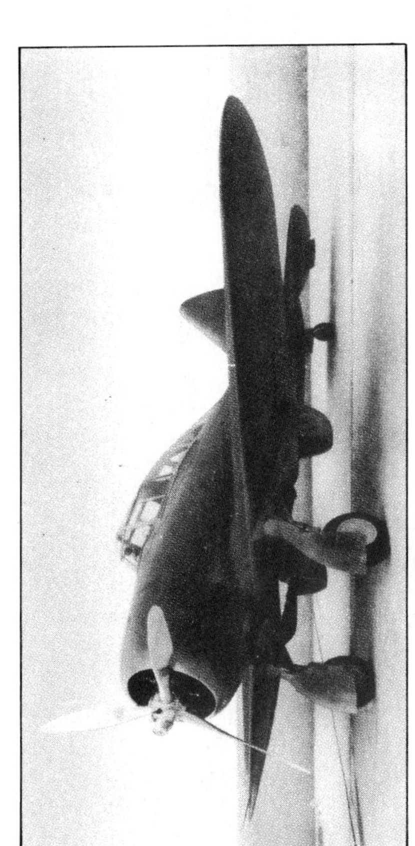

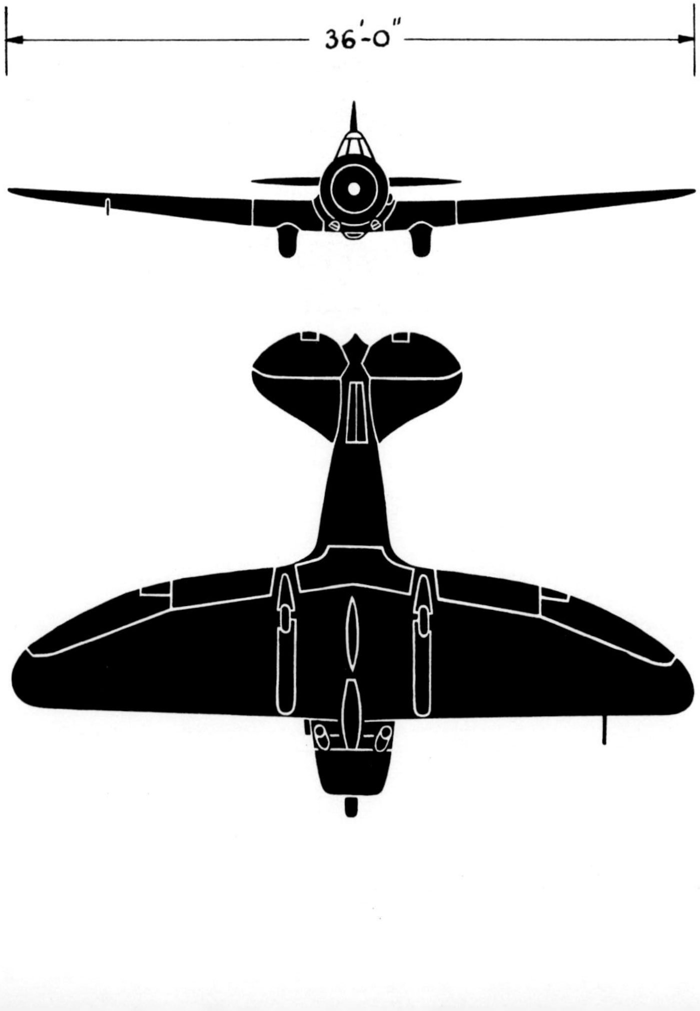

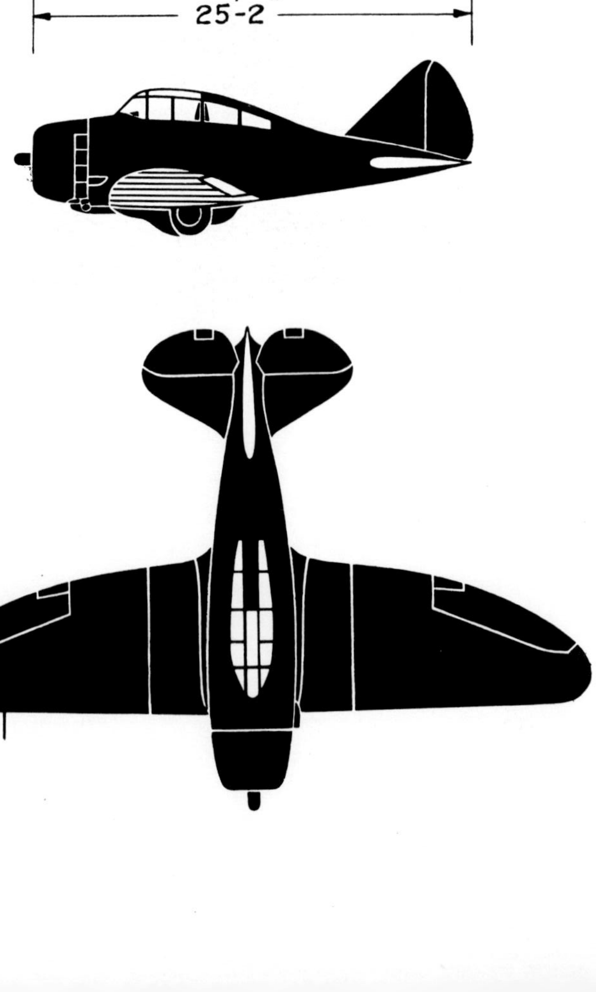

Republic P-35

25'-2"

36'-0"

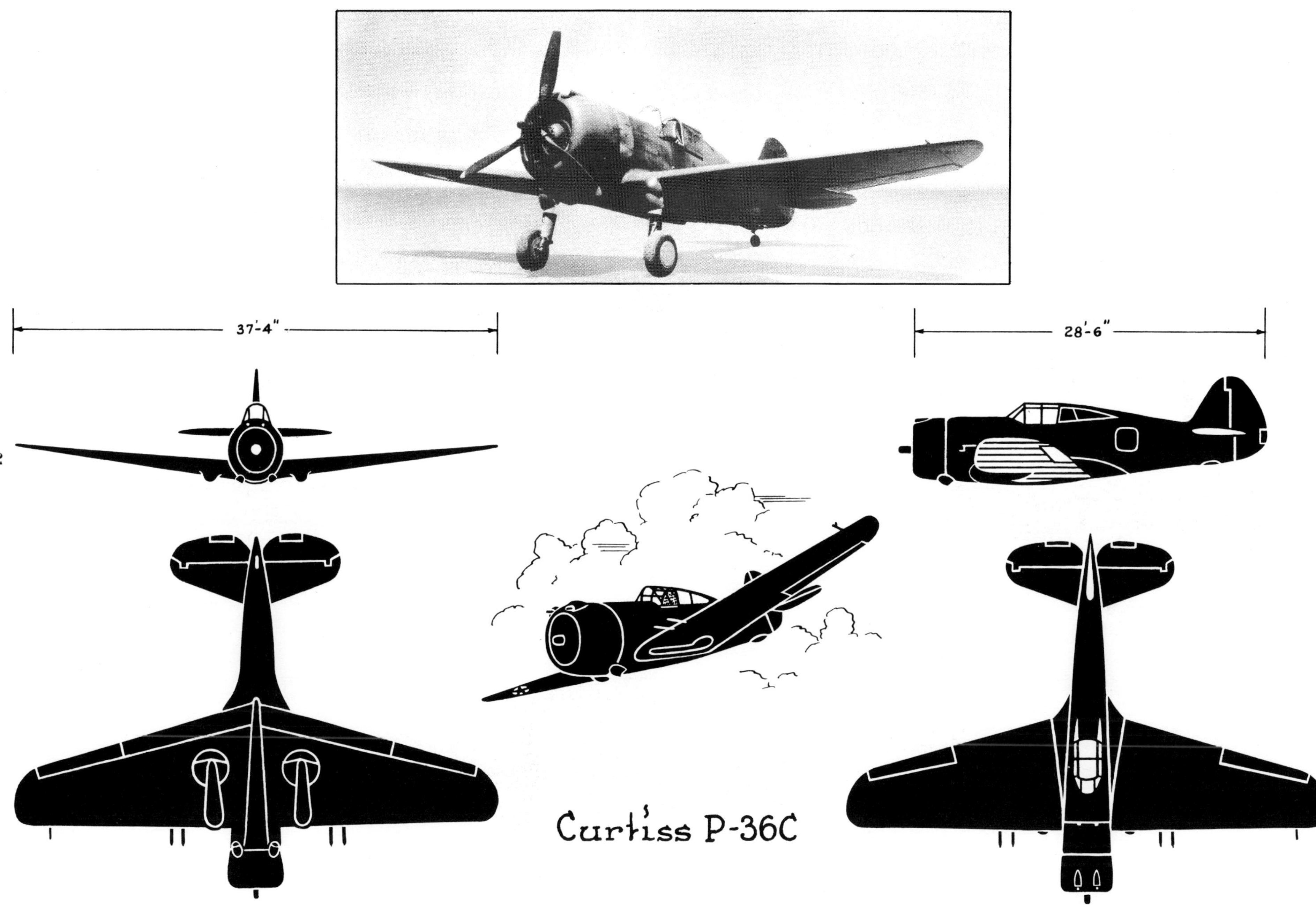
37'-4"
28'-6"
Curtiss P-36C

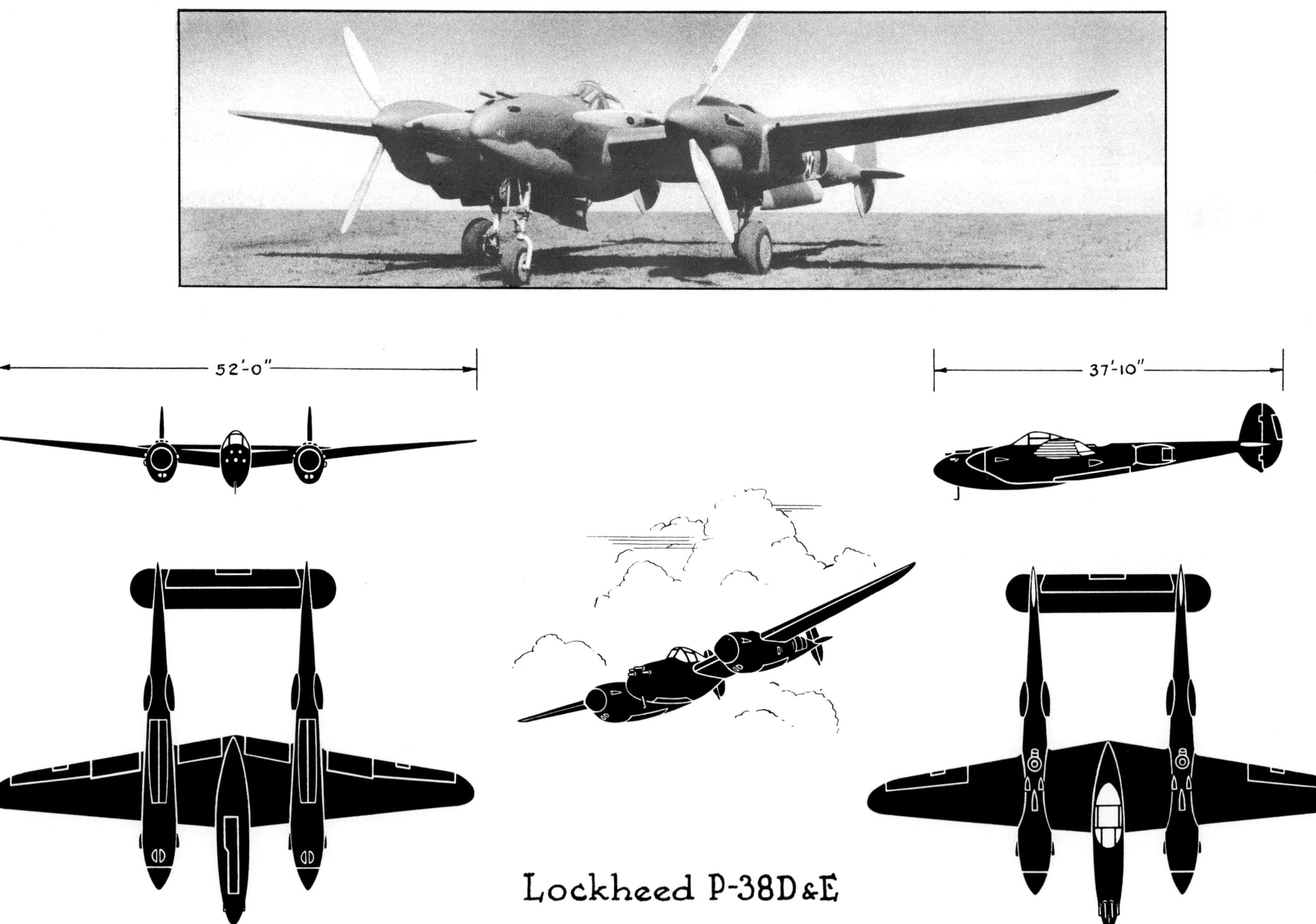
52'-0"
37'-10"
Lockheed P-38D&E

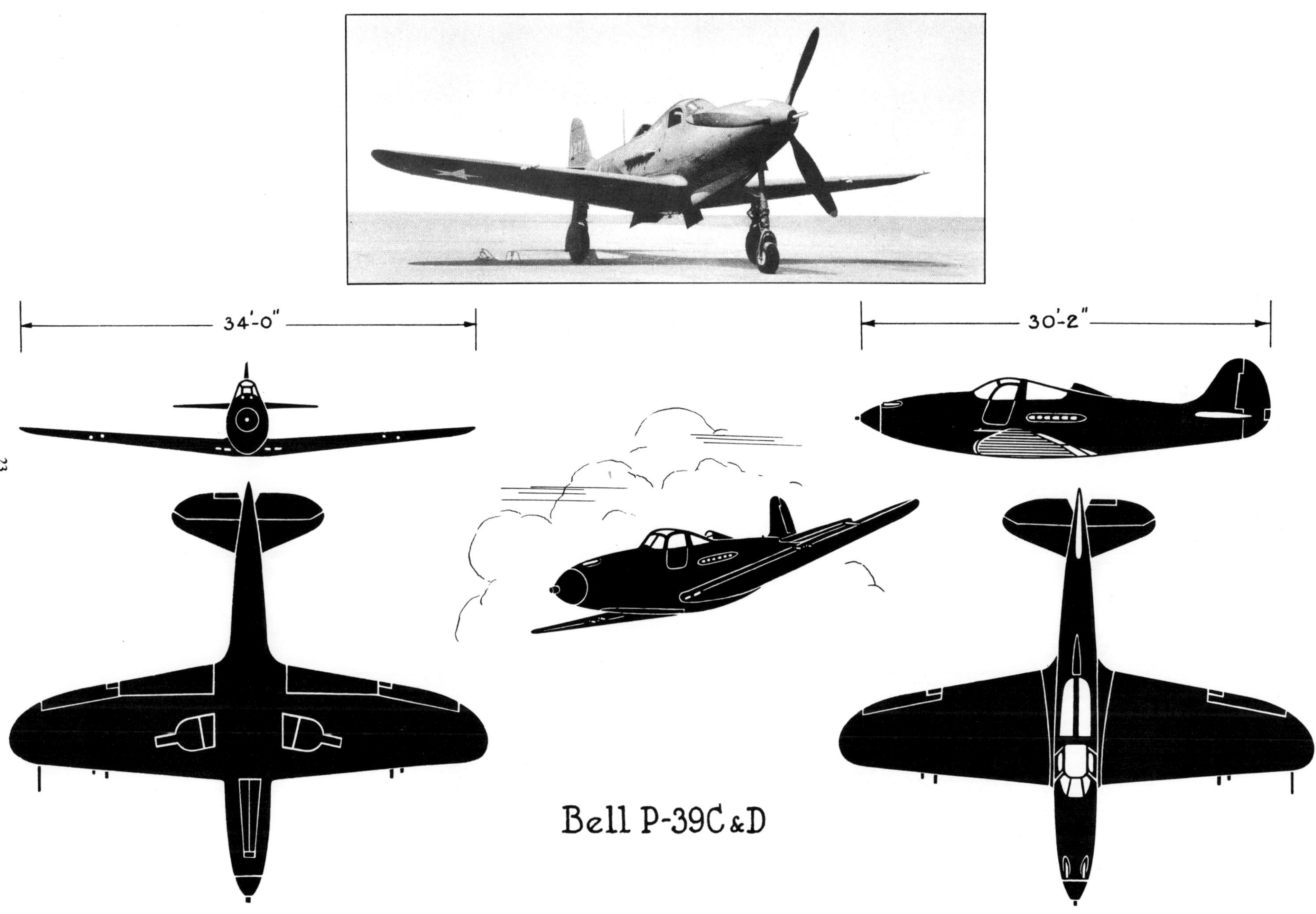


34'-0"
30'-2"
Bell P-39C&D

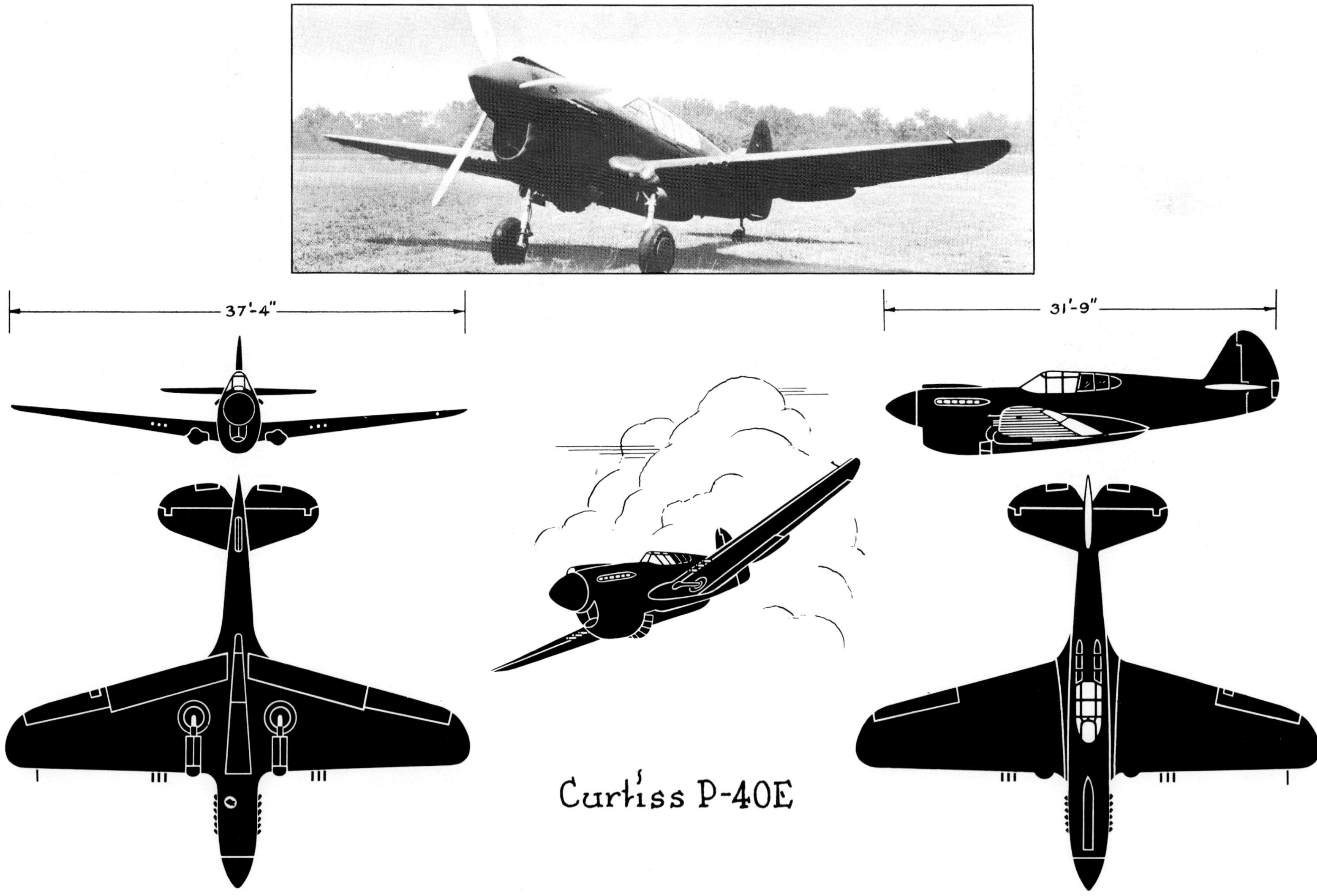


37'-4"
31'-9"
Curtiss P-40E

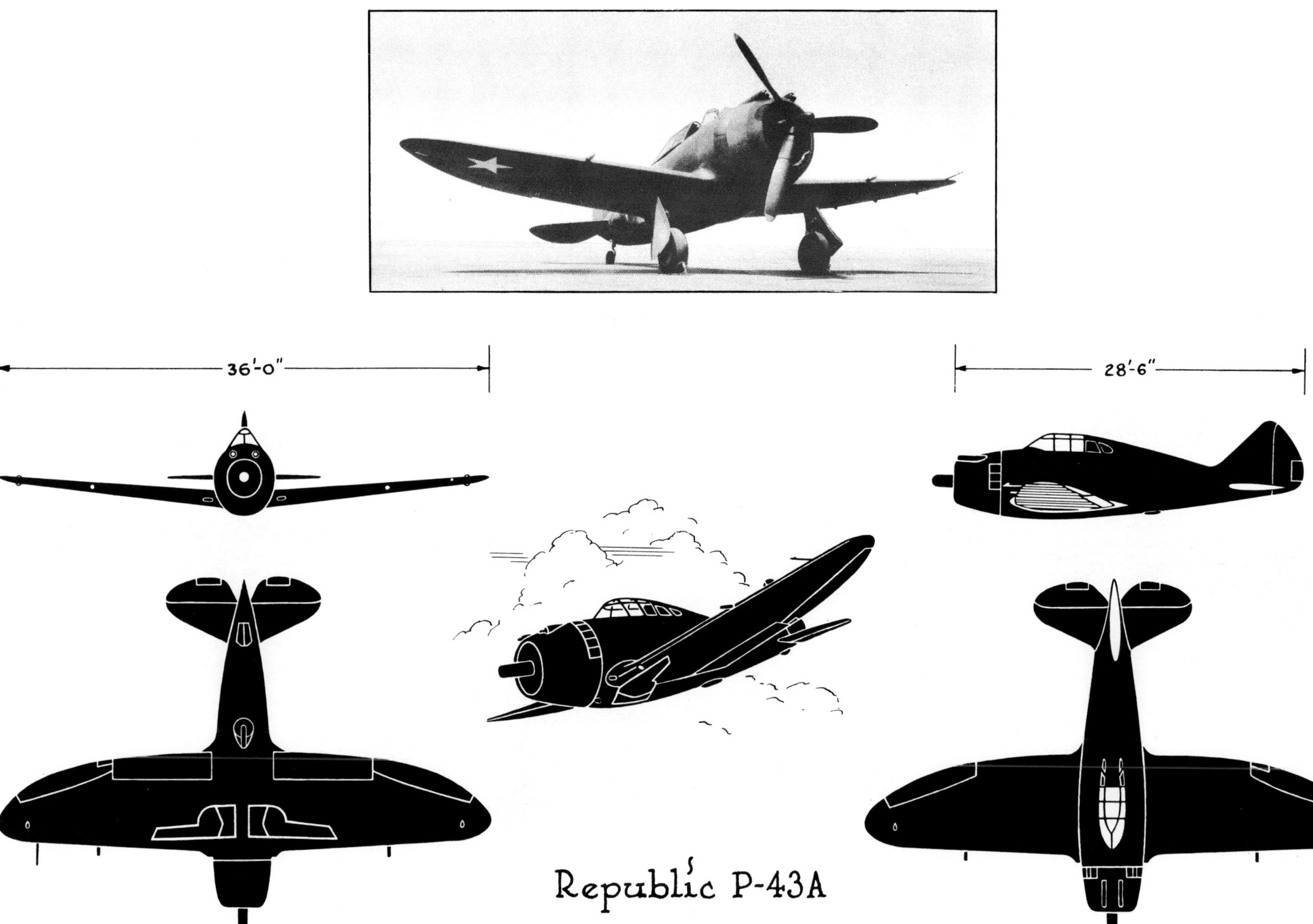


36'-0"
28'-6"
Republic P-43A

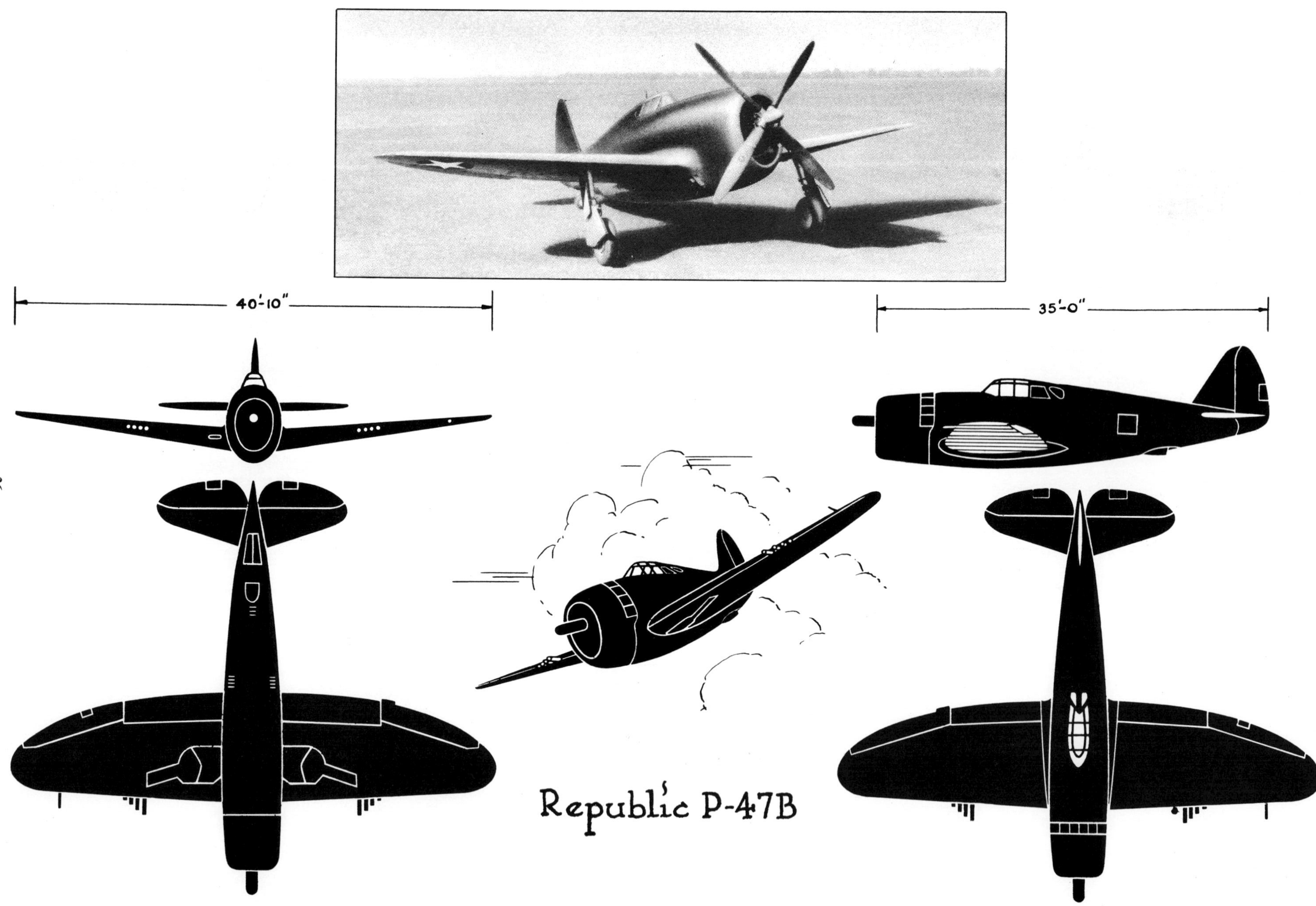


40'-10"
35'-0"
Republic P-47B

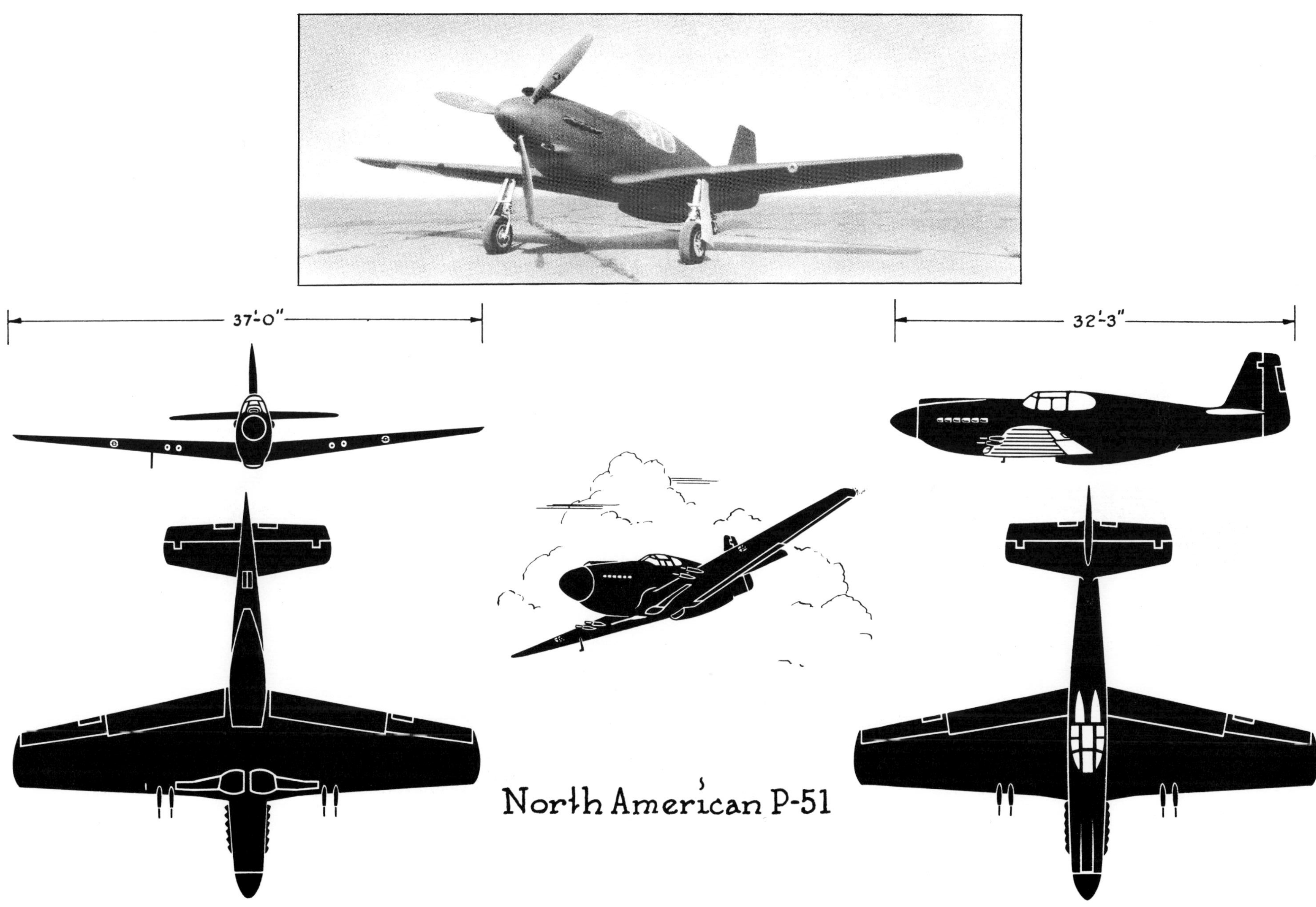

37'-0"
32'-3"
North American P-51

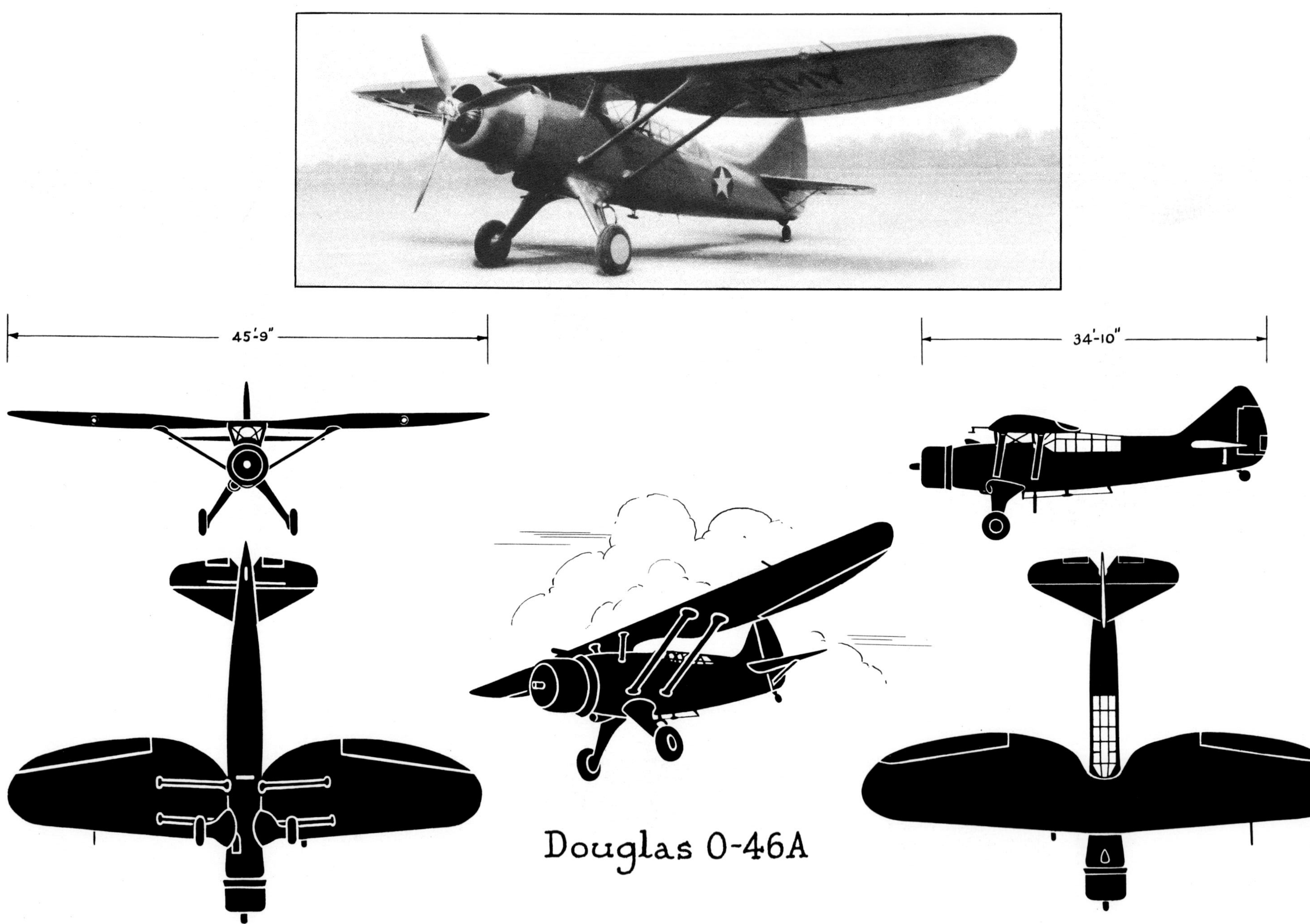

45'-9"
34'-10"
Douglas O-46A

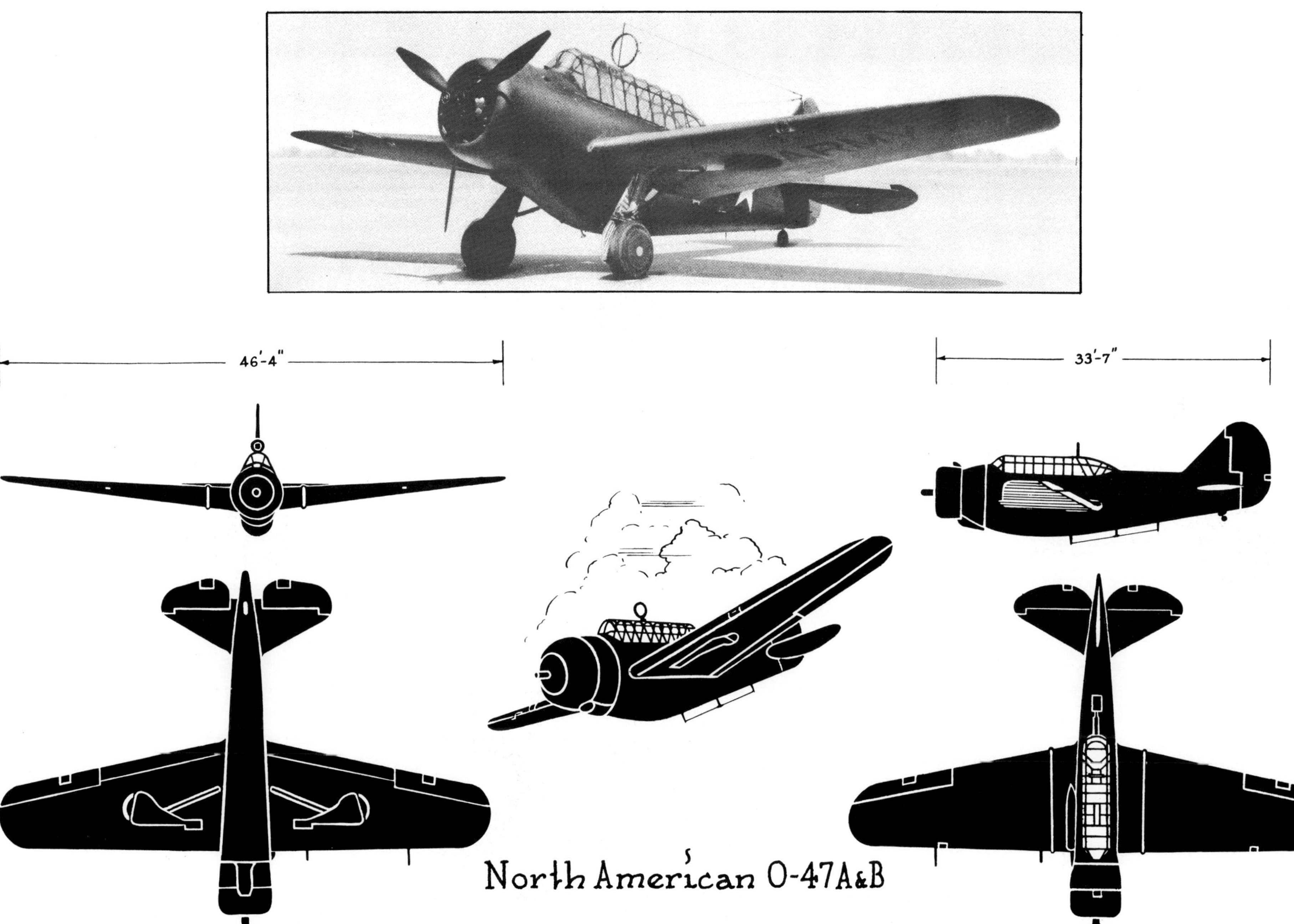

46'-4"
33'-7"
North American O-47A&B

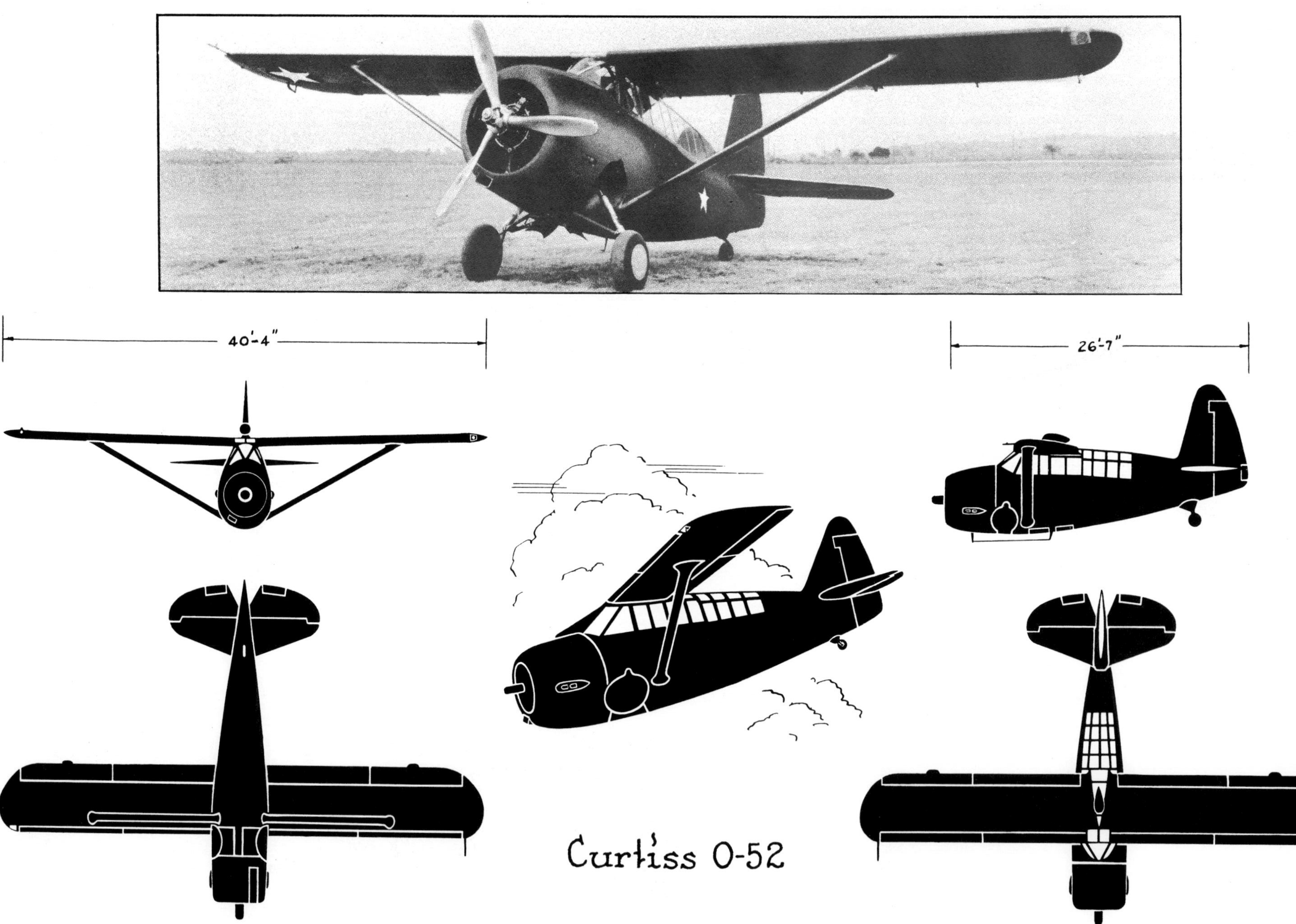


40'-4"
26'-7"
Curtiss O-52

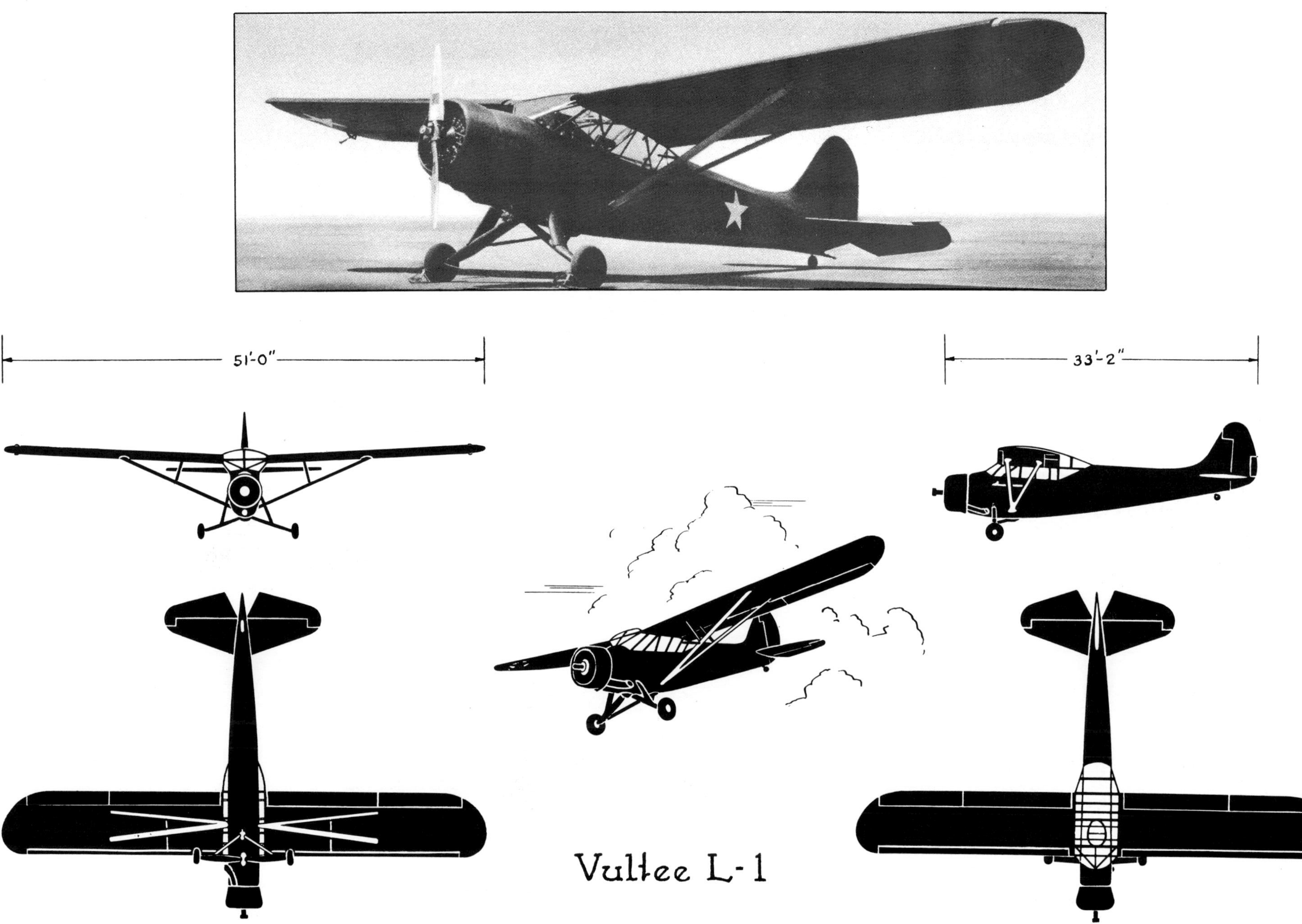

51'-0"
33'-2"
Vultee L-1

49'-0"
38'-8"
Grumman OA-9

104'-0"
64'-0"
Consolidated OA-10

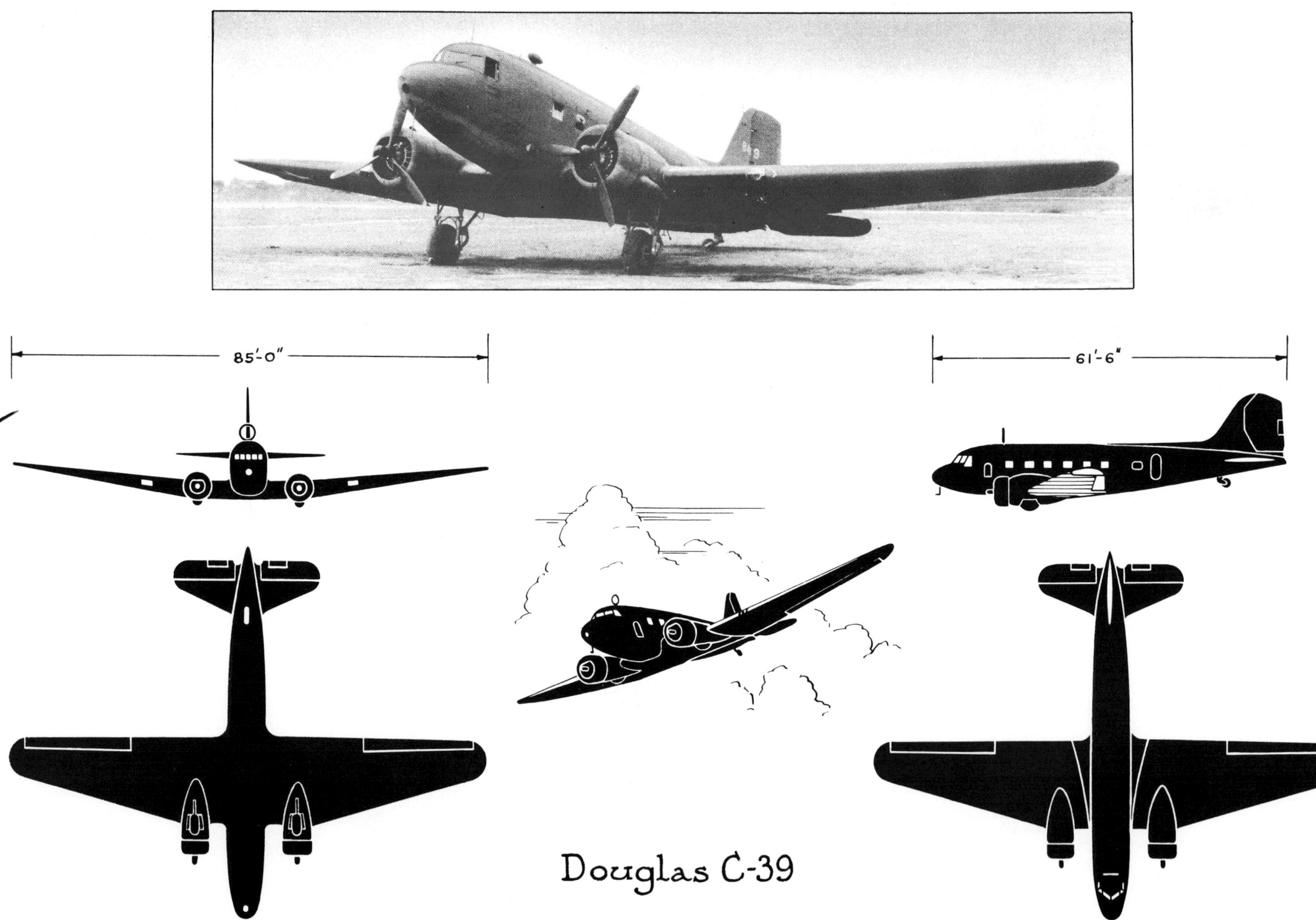
85'-0"
61'-6"
Douglas C-39

49'-6"
36'-4"
Lockheed C-40A

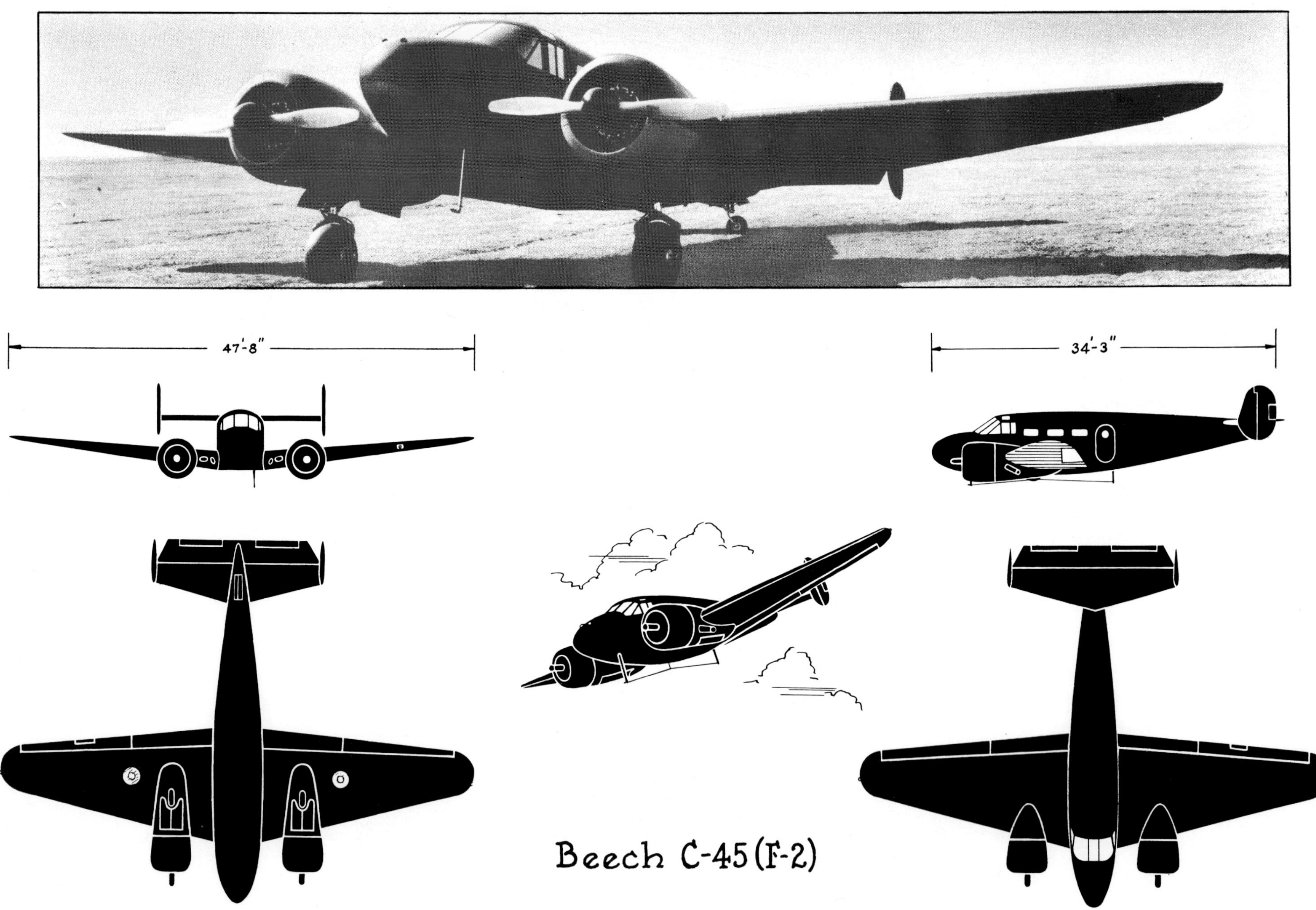


47'-8"
34'-3"
Beech C-45 (F-2)

108'-0"
76'-4"
Curtiss C-46

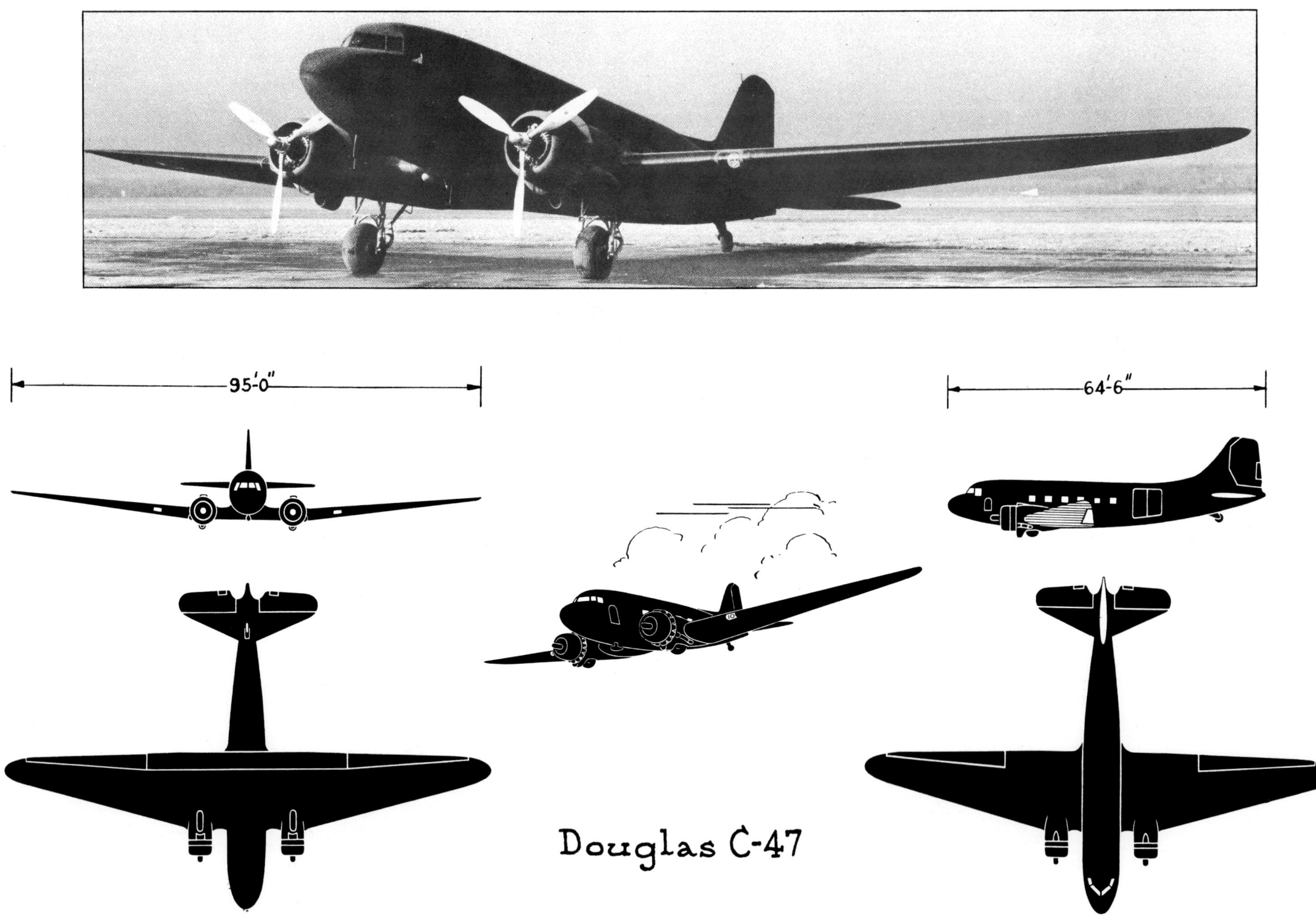

95'-0"
64'-6"
Douglas C-47

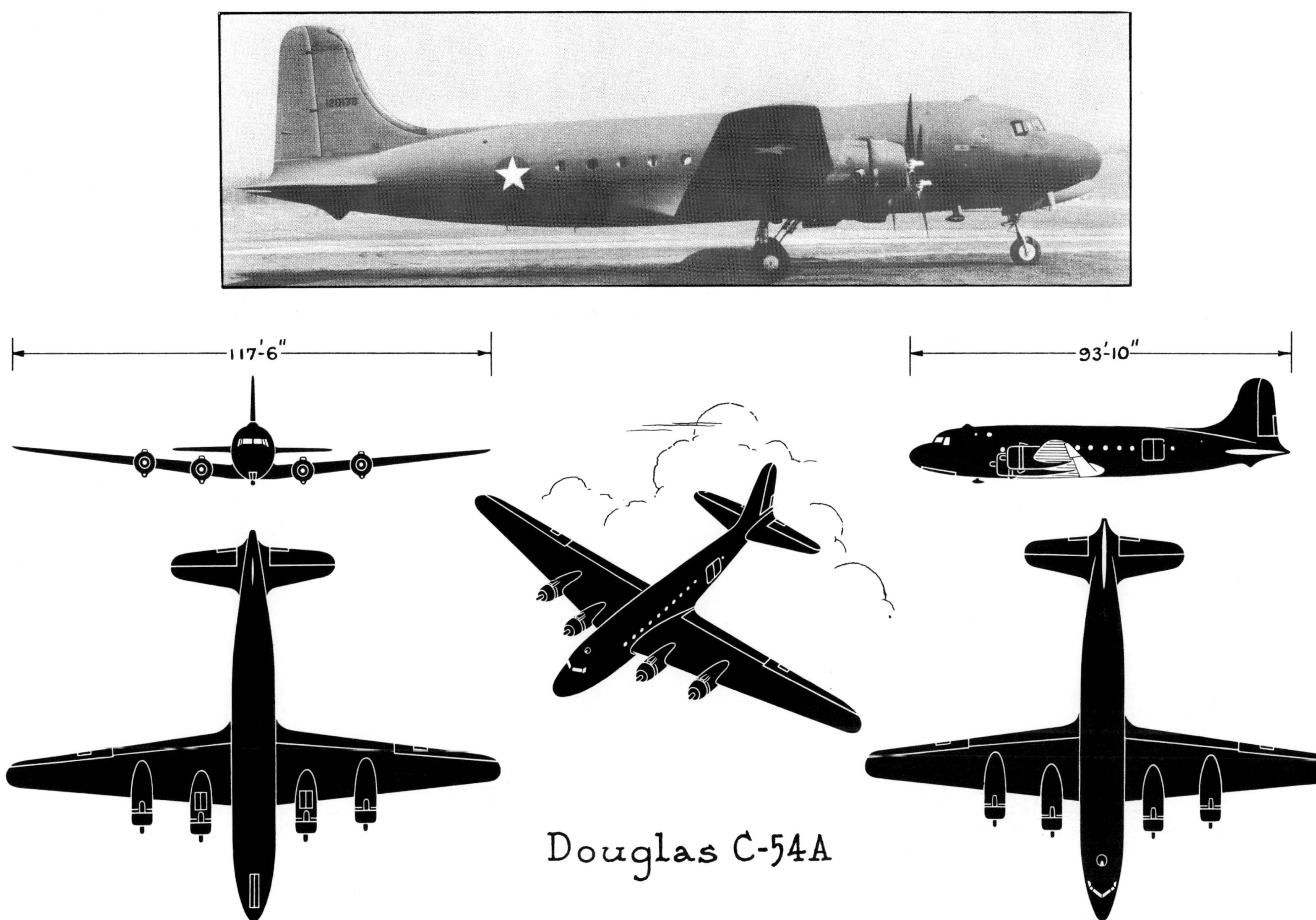
117'-6"
93'-10"
Douglas C-54A

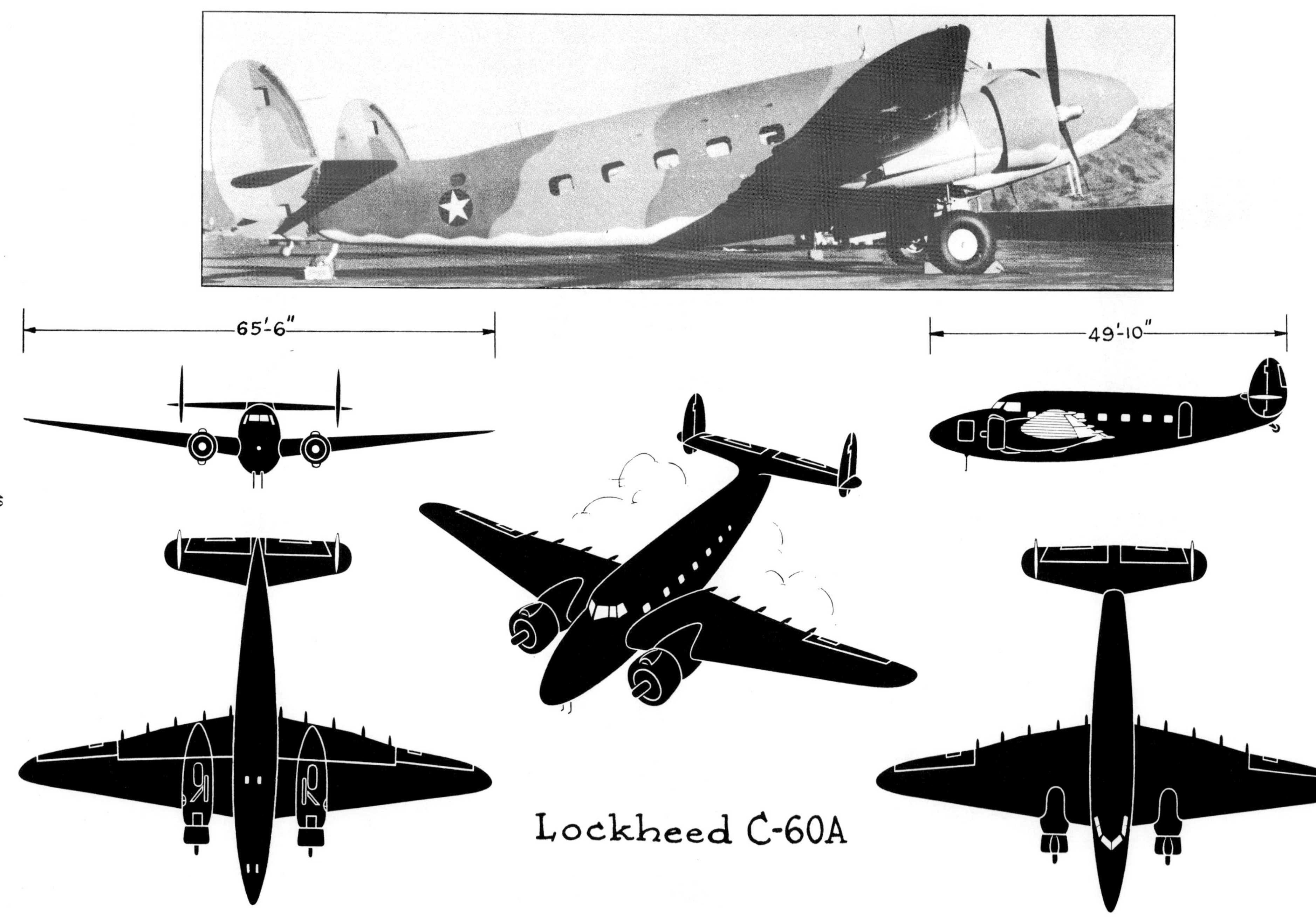

65'-6"
49'-10"
Lockheed C-60A

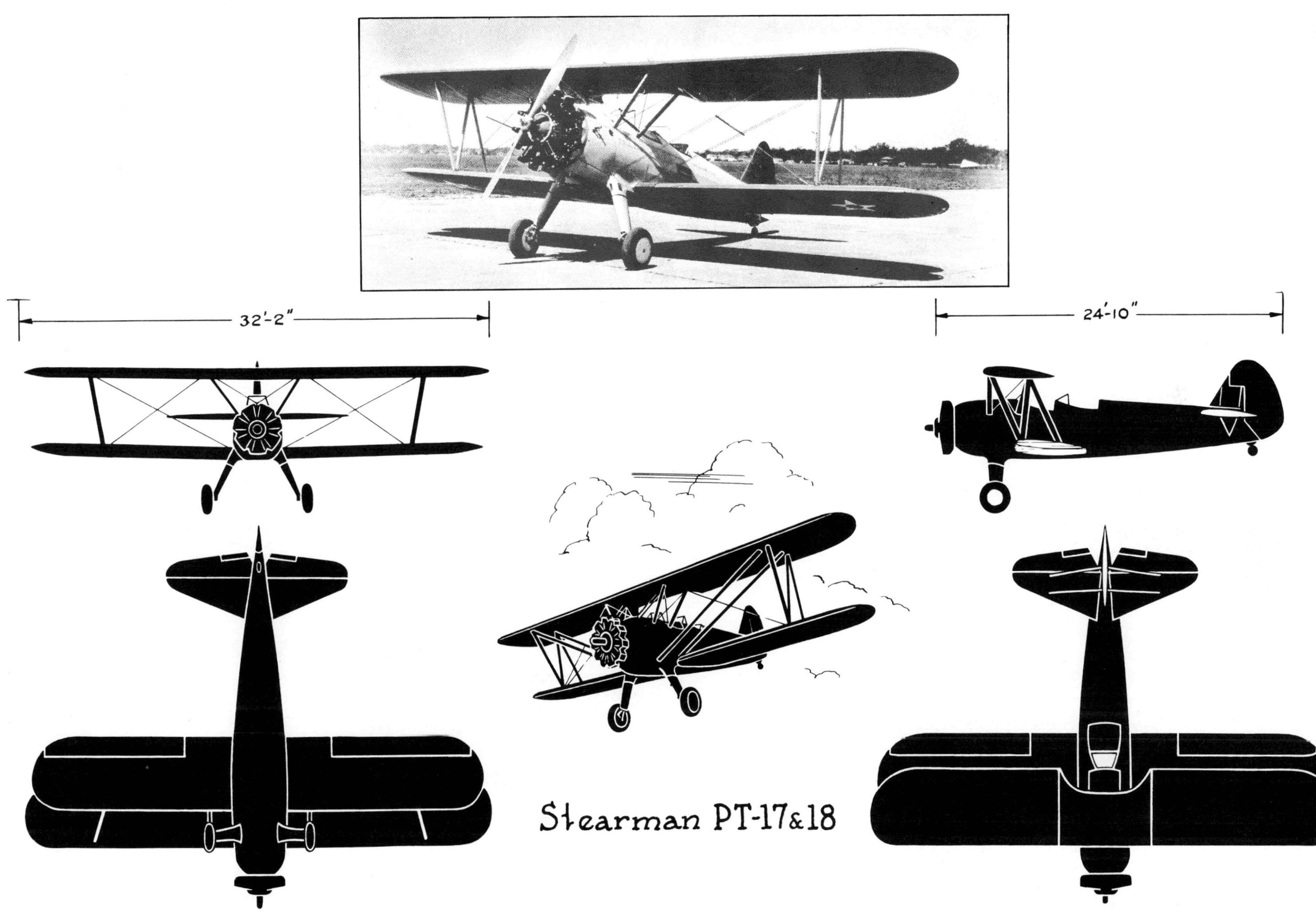


32'-2"
24'-10"
Stearman PT-17&18

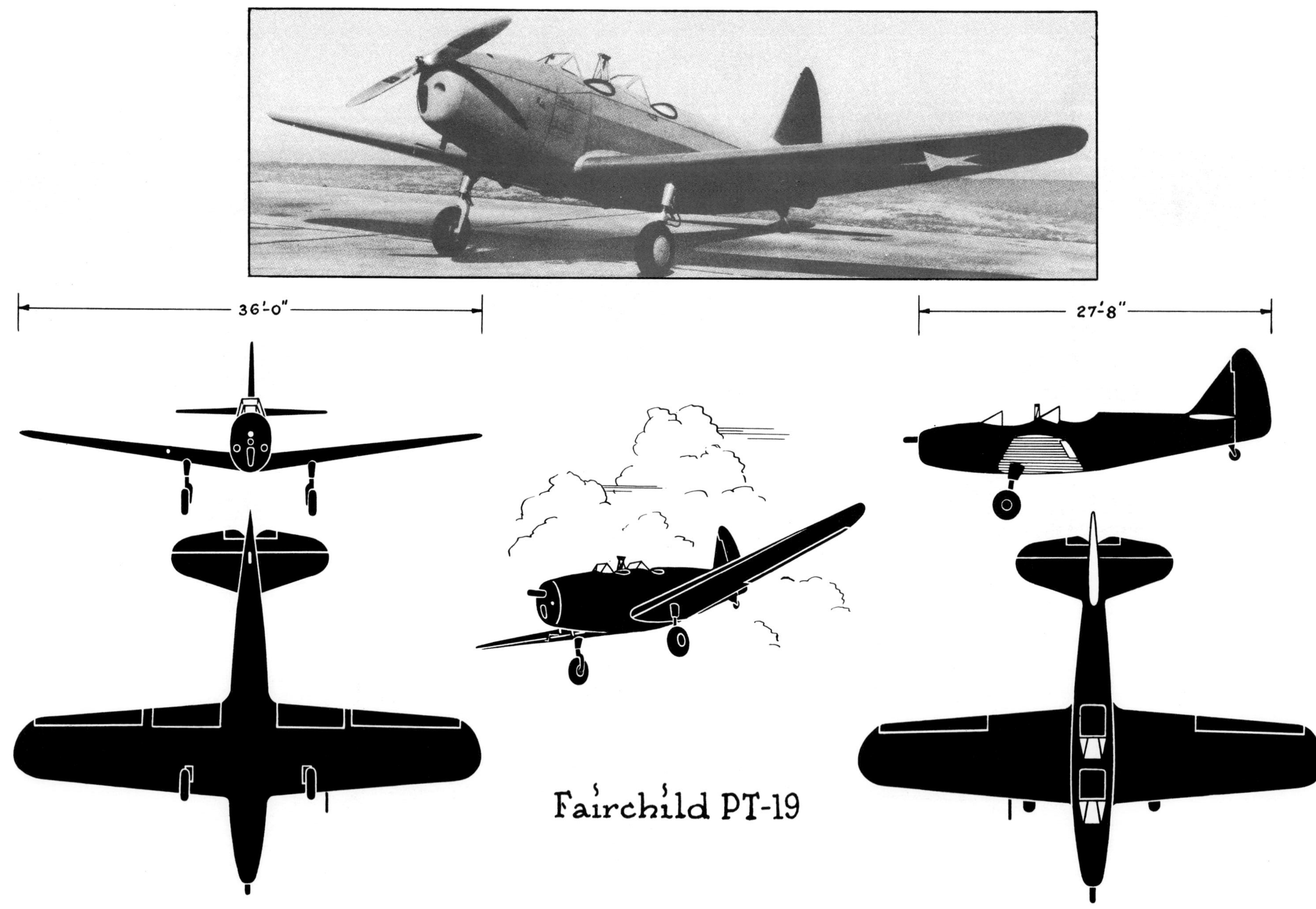

36'-0"
27'-8"
Fairchild PT-19

30'-0"
22'-6"
Ryan PT-22

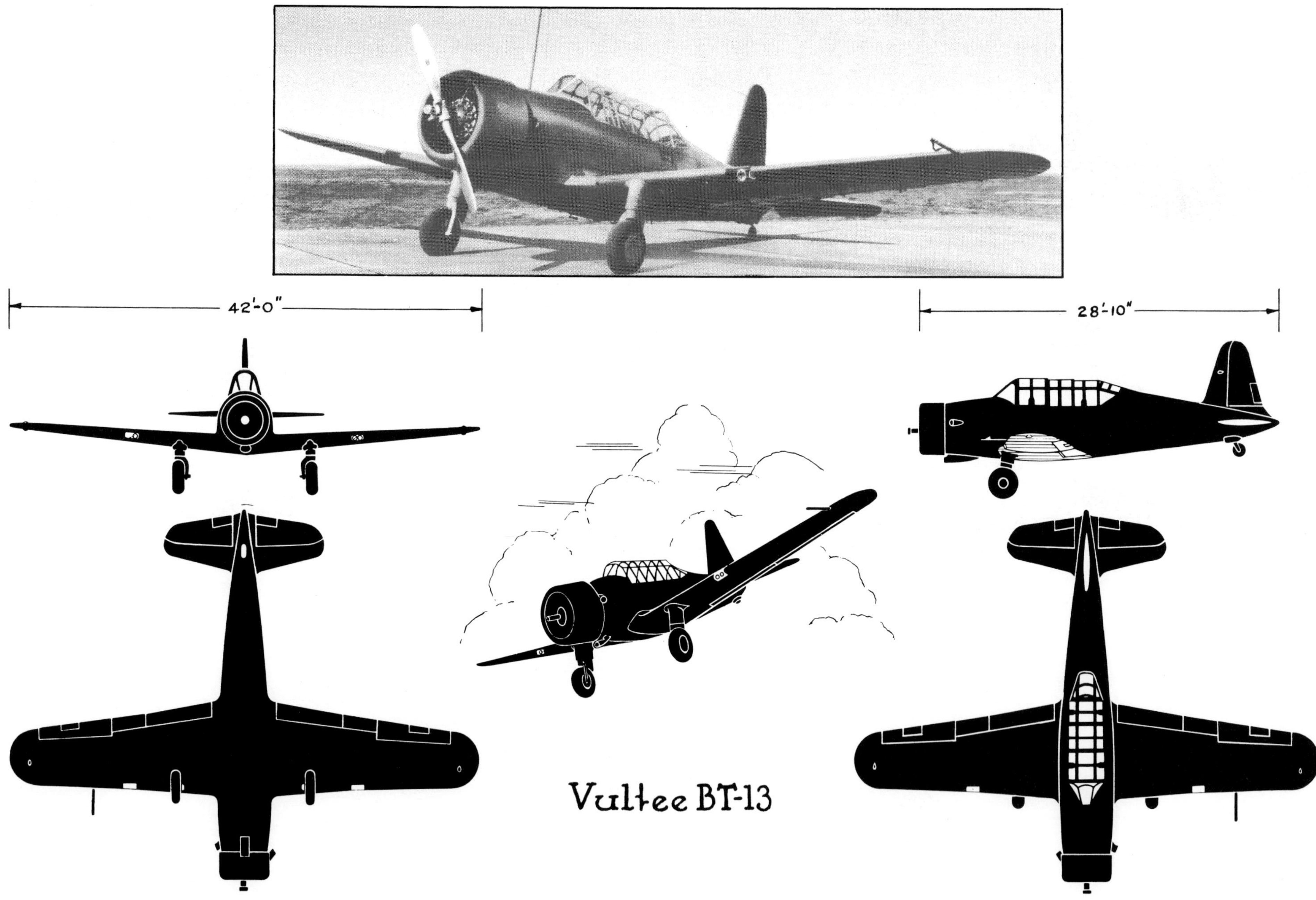


42'-0"
28'-10"
Vultee BT-13

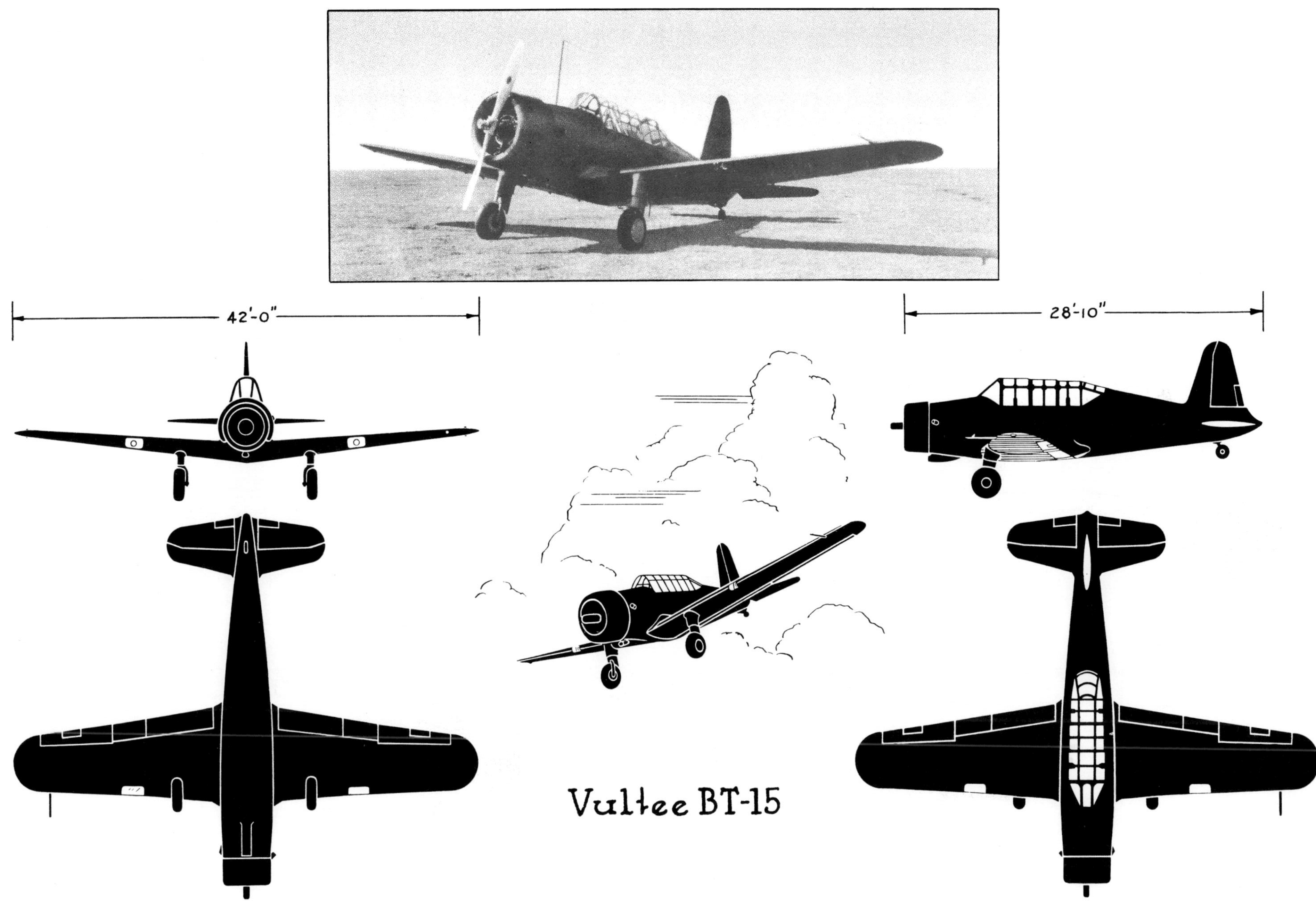

Vultee BT-15

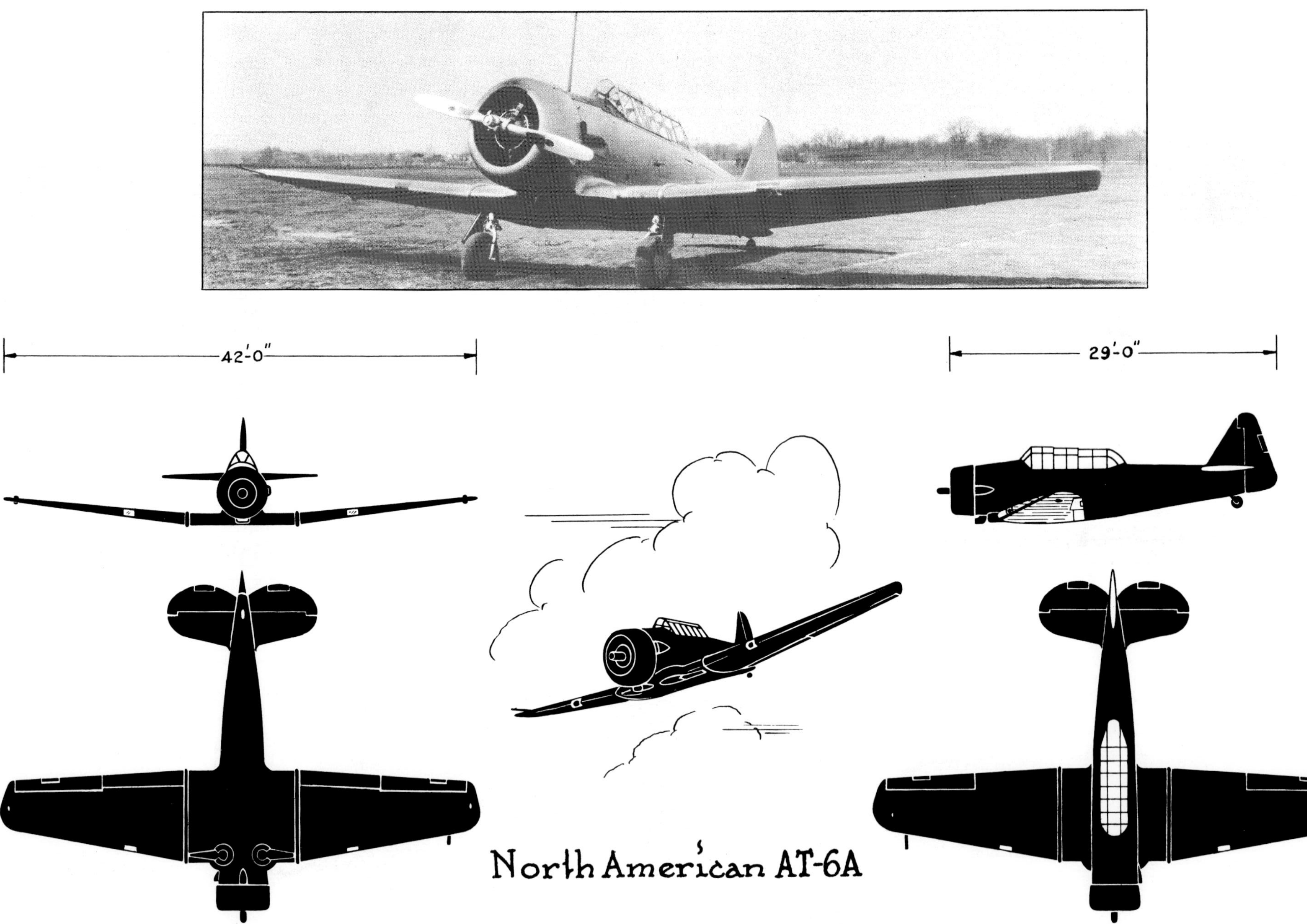


42'-0"
29'-0"
North American AT-6A

47'-8"
34'-3"
Beech AT-7

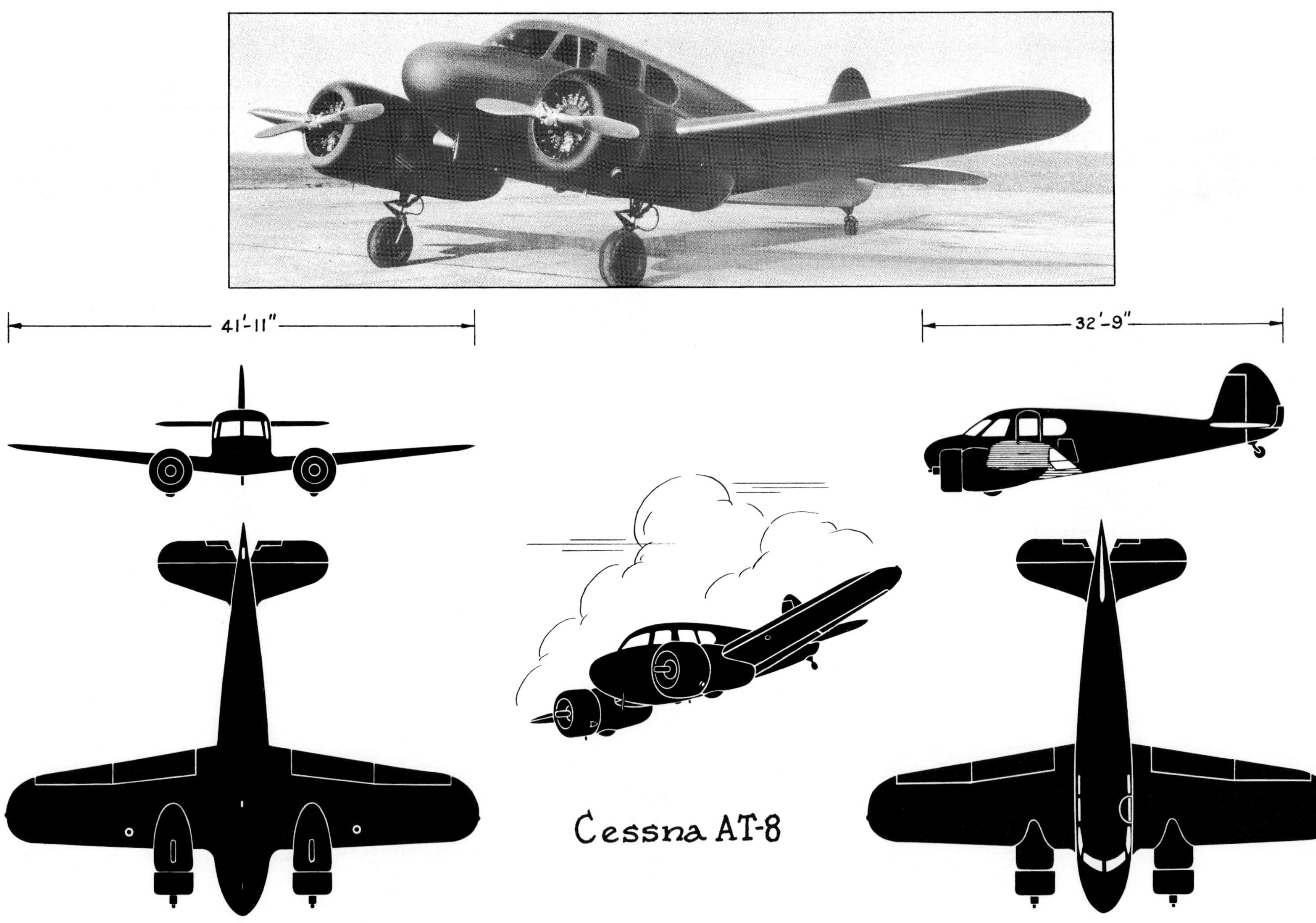


41'-11"
32'-9"
Cessna AT-8

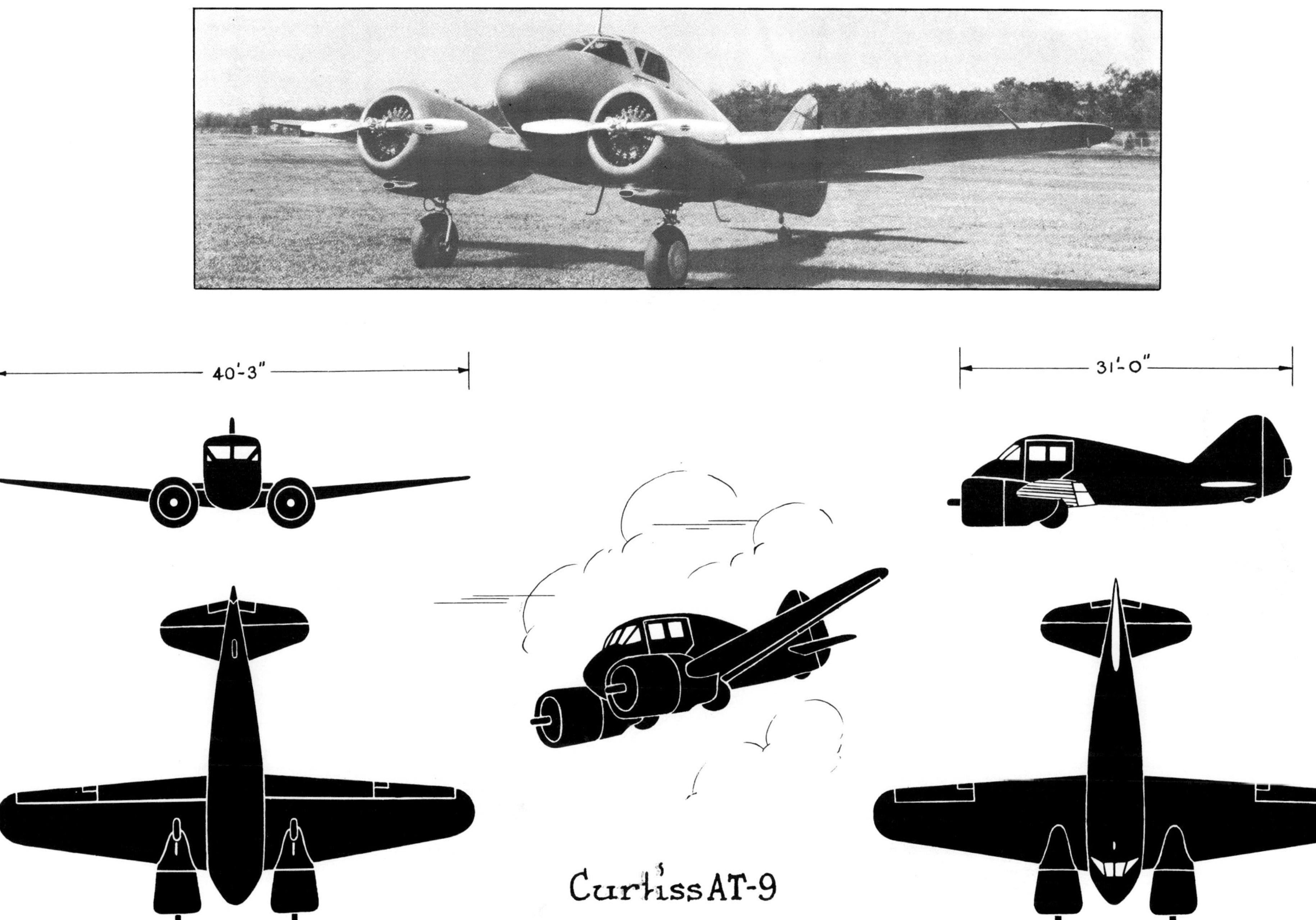


40'-3"
31'-0"
Curtiss AT-9

44'-0"

34'-4"

Beech AT-10

47'-8"
47'-2"
Beech AT-11

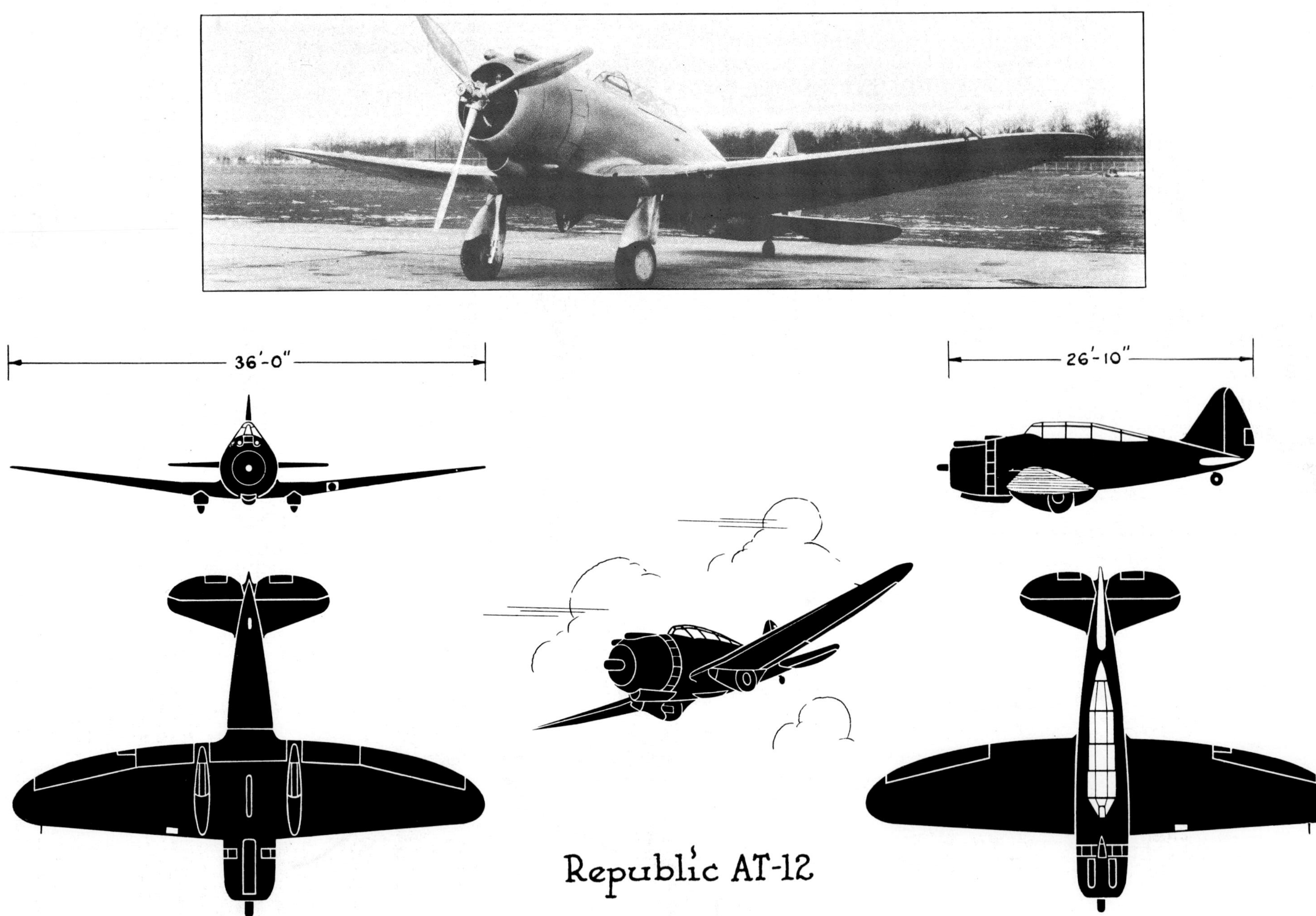

36'-0"
26'-10"
Republic AT-12